Sunny Day Publishing, LLC
Cuyahoga Falls, Ohio 44223
www.sunnydaypublishing.com

The Taste of Freedom Cookbook

ISBN 978-1-948613-15-6
Library of Congress Control Number: 2021952750

LAND OF THE FREE, BECAUSE OF THE BRAVE

OHIO
STANDS
UP!

CHALLENGE ★ HONOR ★ EDUCATE

THE TASTE
OF
FREEDOM!

COOKBOOK

Appetizers

Best Cheese Ball Ever!

Deviled Eggs

Double-Chili Queso Dip

Endive Appetizer

Goat Cheese & Honey Deliciousness

Sausage Dip

Sausage Stuffed Mushroom Caps

Vegetable Pizza

Best Cheese Ball Ever!

INGREDIENTS

2-8 ounce Packages of Cream Cheese

I C Shredded Cheddar Cheese

I tsp Worcestershire

1/4 C Chopped Red Pepper

1/4 C Chopped Red Onion

1/4 C Green Onion (if desired)

3 T Melted Butter

Sprinkle with Black Pepper and Garlic Salt

DIRECTIONS

Mix all together in your blender.

Ensure cheese is softened.

Form with wax paper into a ball.

Serve with Triscuits® or another hearty cracker!

Deviled Eggs

INGREDIENTS

12 Hard Cooked Eggs

1 t salt

1/4 t pepper

2 t prepared mustard

6 T mayonnaise (do not substitute Miracle Whip®)

1 T Olive Oil

4 T sweet relish

1/2 t paprika

DIRECTIONS

My method for the hard boiled eggs is to put eggs in a saucepan and cover with cold water and 1 tablespoon olive oil. Bring eggs to a boil, turn heat off,cover and leave with cover on for 16minutes. With a slotted spoon, take eggs from the saucepan one at a time and crack down on the counter, roll and peel under running cold water. Normally the eggs will peel wonderfully with this method.

After eggs are all peeled, slice eggs in half lengthwise and remove the yolk into a mixing bowl. Add the remaining ingredients to the bowl and mix well so that there are no lumps.

At this point, you can choose to use a spoon to place the mixture into the egg whites or you can use a piping bag with a large tip and squeeze into the hole in the whites.

Sprinkle with additional paprika and place in the refrigerator until ready to serve. Deviled Eggs must be served within 48 hours of preparing.

Barbara H., Uniontown

Double-Chili Queso Dip

INGREDIENTS

1 Small Onion, finely diced

2 Campari® or other small vine-ripened tomatoes (Roma is good)

1/4 C Cilantro (torn/shredded)

1 T Butter

2 Jalapeño Peppers, diced

1/2-1 tsp Salt (according to taste)

1 T All-Purpose Flour

1 C Half & Half Creamer or Milk

1 C Grated Pepper-Jack Cheese

1 C Grated Sharp Cheddar Cheese

1 Bag Tortilla Chips

DIRECTIONS

1.) Combine 1 Tablespoon diced onion, tomatoes, and 1/2 the cilantro in small bowl, set aside

2.) Melt butter in medium saucepan over medium heat, add remaining onion, peppers, and salt; cook; stirring until onions are tender, about 3 minutes

3.) Sprinkle flour into the pan and cook, stirring until completely absorbed, about 1 minute. Whisk in half & half and bring to a simmer; cook, stirring occasionally until slightly thickened, about 4 minutes. Stir in both cheeses until melted, then remove from the heat. Stir in remaining cilantro. Transfer to a bowl and top with tomato-onion mixture. Serve with tortilla chips and enjoy!

Endive Appetizer

- -

SALAD INGREDIENTS

25-30 Single Washed
  Endive Leaves

1 Pack Cranberries, dried

1 Pack Pine Nuts

1 Container Gorgonzola

2 Apples, peeled, cored,
  and chopped

DRESSING INGREDIENTS

2 T Dijon Mustard

4 T Real Maple Syrup

1/4 C Olive Oil

1/4 C Apple Cider
  Vinegar

DIRECTIONS

Mix all filling ingredients and fill each endive leaf.

Combine all dressing ingredients and drizzle dressing over top of salad.

Mary Beth D., Rocky River

Goat Cheese & Honey Deliciousness

INGREDIENTS

One loaf of skinny
French bread

Goat Cheese, softened

Lemon Olive Oil
(easily made with 1/3
cup EVOO and juice of
one small lemon, mixed)

1/3 C Honey

DIRECTIONS

Slice bread in 1/4- 1/2 inch diagonals.

Lightly toast in at oven at 300°F for 5 to 7
minutes. Let it cool.

Gently cover the top of the bread with
softened goat cheese (don't treat it like a
sandwich, a little heavier and not perfectly
spread makes for a nicer look)

Lightly drizzle Honey over the top

Lightly drizzle lemon olive oil over the top

Place on a dish with delicate greens cover-
ing the toast points!

Sausage Dip

INGREDIENTS

* 2 lbs Sausage

* 2-8 oz Packages
  Cream Cheese

* 2-4 oz Cans of Green
  Chiles

* 1 Bag Tortilla Chips

DIRECTIONS

1. In a 2 quart crock-pot add in sausage & cook until brown on high.

2. Add in cream cheese. Mix well until softened.

3. Strain green chiles & add to crock-pot. Mix well. Reduce heat to low.

4. Serve with tortilla chips.

Note: Use any type of corn chips as an alternative.

Sausage Stuffed Mushroom Caps

INGREDIENTS

I lb Fresh Mushrooms
  (about 20)

1/2 lb Bulk Pork Sausage

2 T Chopped Onion

I C Bread Crumbs

I tsp Parsley

1/2 tsp Black Pepper

DIRECTIONS

Clean mushrooms, scoop out caps and chop stems fine.

Sauté sausage and drain; add chopped stems and onions and cook a few minutes.

Add 2 tablespoons water and remaining ingredients.

Mix with fingers. Fill mushroom caps with sausage mixture.

To shallow baking pan; add 2 tablespoons water and mushroom caps and bake at 375 degrees F for 15 minutes.

Vegetable Pizza

INGREDIENTS

2 Tubes Refrigerated Crescent Rolls

2 8 oz Packages Cream Cheese Softened

1 C Hellmann's® Mayonnaise

1 Package Hidden Valley® Ranch dressing (dry)

DIRECTIONS

Spread crescent rolls on cookie sheet and bake 10 min using temp on package.

Mix and spread the cream cheese, mayonnaise, and ranch packet on top of dough.

Add the following toppings to the pizza in any order:

1 C Diced Green Peppers
1 C Broccoli
1 C Cauliflower
(Any other veggies you want...I have used cucumbers, black olives, garbanzo beans, zucchini, peas...etc.)

2 C Shredded Cheddar/Mozzarella Cheese mixture

Best if chilled overnight

Sharon C. G.

Breakfast

Breakfast Burritos

Easter Morning Almond Pecan Danish

Fluffy Fall Pancakes

Kathy's Griddle Cakes

Breakfast Burritos

- -

DIRECTIONS

Place in a large skillet and saute:

> 2 T Oil

> 2 Cloves Garlic, finely minced

> 1 Onion, finely diced

> 1 Green Pepper, finely diced

Add and cook until done:

> 1 lb. Bulk Sausage

Place in medium mixing bowl and beat with egg beater or fork:

> 12 Eggs, beaten

> 1/2 tsp Salt

> 1/4 tsp Black Pepper, ground

> 6 T Half-and-Half or (1/4 c. cream & 1/4 c. water)

Meanwhile place on medium heat a large nonstick skillet:

> 2 T Butter or Oil

Swirl to coat the bottom, pour in the egg mixture constantly stirring, slowly pushing from side to side, scraping along bottom of skillet lifting and folding eggs as they form curds. Do not over-scramble, as curds formed will be too small. Cook eggs until large curds form but eggs are still very moist, 2-3 minutes. Turn heat to low and add:

> 1/2 C Chunky Salsa (your choice of heat)

> 2 C/8 oz Cheddar Cheese, shredded

> 1 Small Can Green Chilies, drained, chopped

Breakfast Burritos (continued)

- -

Jalapeno Slices - # of your choice, optional

2 Green Onions, sliced with tops, optional

Use a potato masher to get egg chunks in a smaller size. Remove from heat and combine with sausage mixture. Warm in microwave 30 seconds 3 at a time between paper towels:

15 - 20 Tortillas, large

Use a #16 scoop and place 2 scoops (1/2 c. total) egg mixture into tortilla; roll burrito-style.

FREEZING

Put burritos in single layer on silicone or parchment or lightly greased cookie sheets. When fully frozen, wrap burritos individually; place wrapped burritos in large zip-top freezer bags; freeze. A family favorite these disappear quickly at our house!

TO SERVE

Unwrap burritos from foil or plastic wrap that you used for freezing. Wrap in a paper towel. Cook in microwave until heated through (about 2 minutes). Or thaw burritos (remove plastic wrap if used in freezing), wrap burritos in foil, and bake at 350 degrees for ten minutes.

Take these camping, place the bag of frozen burritos in the ice chest, and by the first morning they are fully thawed. Simply reheat them in a large skillet over the camp stove or fire grate.

Easter Morning Almond Pecan Danish

INGREDIENTS

Bottom layer

1 C All-Purpose Flour

1/2 C Softened Butter

2 T Water

Top layer

1 C Water

1 tsp Almond Extract

1/2 C Softened Butter/ Margarine

1 C All-Purpose Flour

3 Eggs

Top layer

1 C Powdered Sugar

1 tsp Almond Extract

1/2 C Pecan Pieces

DIRECTIONS

Preheat oven to 350 degrees.

To make bottom layer, with a fork, cut 1/2 cup softened butter into the 1 cup of all-purpose flour until mixture combines into small pea size balls. Mix in 2 tablespoons of water until dough can be patted into a ball. Don't be afraid to add a little more flour if dough is too moist, or a little more water if dough is too dry. Dough should be easy to form into a ball. Divide the ball into two halves and press each half into an 11 by 3 inch rectangle on a large ungreased baking sheet (making 2 side by side rectangles).

For the top layer, bring 1 cup water and 1/2 cup butter to a boil in a medium saucepan over high heat. Remove from heat. Immediately add the almond extract and 1 cup flour. Return the pan to low heat and stir continuously until a ball forms in 1 to 2 minutes. Remove again from heat and beat in the 3 eggs until mixture becomes glossy. Spread this layer evenly over the two rectangles and bake 1 hour or until the top layer is a golden brown.

As the two rectangles cool, watch them transform into a flaky, yet creamy custard loaf.

Top the two cooled loaves with an almond icing made by stirring about 1 to 2 tablespoon of warm water and 1 teaspoon of almond extract into 1 cup powdered sugar until it can be spooned over the loaves. Top with pecan pieces.

When icing sets up, cut loaves into strips.

Makes fourteen 1-1/2 by 3 inch strips.

"This is a delicious light Easter breakfast with a bowl of strawberries and a glass of mimosa or orange juice. Enjoy!"

Tom St. A.

Fluffy Fall Pancakes

- -

INGREDIENTS

2 eggs

2 cups all-purpose flour

1 cup milk

4 Tbsp canola oil

6 tsp baking powder

1 tsp salt

3 Tbsp sugar

1 cup applesauce

Pinch of ginger

1 tsp cinnamon

1/2 tsp ground cloves

1/4 tsp ground nutmeg

DIRECTIONS

Mix all ingredients together.

Heat skillet on medium, and melt some butter on it.

Flip the pancakes when they start to bubble.

Enjoy!

Kathy's Griddle Cakes

INGREDIENTS

2 C Flour, sifted

4 tsp Baking Powder

1 tsp Salt

4 T sugar

2 Large Eggs

1 C Milk

4 T Vegetable Oil

1/2 tsp Cinnamon

DIRECTIONS

In a large bowl, mix together sugar, salt, eggs, and oil. Add flour, baking powder, cinnamon, and milk. Mix well.

Drop by tablespoons on hot, greased griddle.

Cook several minutes until light brown.

Flip and cook until firm.

Kathy L., Akron, Ohio

Soups & Chilis

Baked Potato Soup

Best Potato Soup

Beef Vegetable Soup

Broccoli Cheese Soup

Cincinnati Chili

Clam Chowder

Quick Green Chili

Succotash Soup

The Best Quick Chili EVER

Baked Potato Soup

INGREDIENTS

4 Large Baking Potatoes

2/3 C (about 10 T) Butter

2/3 C Flour

6 C Milk

3/4 tsp Salt

1/2 tsp Pepper

4 Green Onions, chopped

1 Jar Bacon Bits

1-1/4 C Shredded Cheddar Cheese

8 oz. Sour Cream

DIRECTIONS

Wash potatoes and prick with a fork. Bake at 400 degrees F for 1 hour. Cool. Remove majority of potato peels from pulp, leaving some peel for color. Roughly chop and mash the pulp. Sit potato aside.

Melt butter in a heavy pot over low heat. Add flour and stir until smooth. Cook and stir 1 minute. Gradually stir in milk, whisking until thick and bubbly.

Stir in potato pulp, salt, pepper, half of the green onions, half of the bacon bits, and 1 cup of cheese. Heat and stir until mixture is smooth and cheese is melted. Stir in sour cream and heat briefly. Pass remaining bacon bits and cheese at the table.

Extra cheese, onions, and bacon can be added to recipe for those who like stronger flavors. Serve with salad and homemade bread!

Lisa M., Streetsboro

Best Potato Soup

INGREDIENTS

4-6 medium potatoes

1/2 pack Chicken or Ham lunch meat

4 cups water

1 heaping Tbsp Better Than Bouillon®

1/2 tsp salt

1 tsp garlic pepper

5 Tbsp butter

5 Tbsp flour

2-1/2 cups milk

Shredded cheddar cheese, bacon, and scallions for topping (optional

DIRECTIONS

Combine potatoes, meat, and water in Dutch Oven pot and bring to boil. Reduce to medium heat and cook 10-15 minutes. Mix in Better Than Bouillon®, salt, and garlic pepper.

In a separate small pot, melt the butter on medium heat. Whisk in the flour, stirring constantly. Slowly add in the milk and whisk 3-4 minutes until thickened. Add the milk rue into the main pot and heat through to serve. Pairs wonderfully with pretzel rolls.

Beef Vegetable Soup

INGREDIENTS

1 LB Ground Beef - Browned

1-1/4 C Chopped Onions

2 C Sliced Carrots

1 C Chopped Green Pepper

3 Stalks Celery Slices

2 Cans of Corn

1 46 oz Can Tomato Juice

2 tsp Sugar

1 tsp Celery Seed

Salt & Pepper to taste

DIRECTIONS

Mix ingredients together. Bring to a Boil. Reduce heat and simmer for 30 minutes, stirring occasionally.

Can be frozen and reheated to eat at a later time.

Barbara H., Uniontown

Broccoli Cheese Soup

INGREDIENTS

1 Box Frozen Chopped
  Broccoli

3 C Water

1/3 C Finely Chopped
  Onion

1 T Butter

1 T Chicken Base

1/2 tsp Garlic Salt

1/2 tsp Black Pepper

1 Can Cream of
  Mushroom Soup

15 oz Fine Noodles

3/4 lb White American
  cheese

3 C Whole milk

DIRECTIONS

Thaw broccoli in boiling water, add remaining ingredients in order listed above, allowing noodles to soften before adding cheese and milk.

Cook until heated through and noodles are done, stirring frequently.

Cincinnati Chili
Makes 8 to 10 servings

DIRECTIONS

Place in a saucepan and combine:

> 2 lb Ground Beef
>
> 2 Medium Onions, chopped
>
> 1 Quart Water

Simmer until beef turns brown. Add:

> 16 oz Can Tomatoes
>
> 1-1/2 tsp Vinegar
>
> 1 tsp Worcestershire Sauce
>
> 1 T Chili Powder
>
> 2 tsp Cumin, ground
>
> 1-1/2 tsp Allspice, ground
>
> 1-1/2 tsp Salt
>
> 1 tsp Cayenne
>
> 1 tsp Cinnamon, ground
>
> 1/2 tsp Garlic Powder
>
> 2 Bay Leaves

Cover; simmer 3 hours. The fat will float. If there is time, chill chili and lift off fat layer or spoon off fat.

To serve - basic "three-way chili," serve chili on:

Cooked spaghetti, hot, 6 servings

Cincinnati Chili (continued)

--- -- -- -- -- --- -- -- --- -- -- -- -- -- -

And top with:

     1-1/2 C Cheddar Cheese, shredded, 6 servings

Pass:

     12 oz Oyster Crackers, 6 servings

"four-way chili" add:

     1 C Onion, chopped, 6 servings

"five-way chili" add:

     16 oz Kidney Beans, heated, 6 servings

Clam Chowder

- -

INGREDIENTS

2 Medium White
   Potatoes (use sweet
   potatoes for variety)

1 Medium Onion

1 Stalk Celery

2 T Butter

1 Can Minced Clams

Large pinch Cayenne
   Red Pepper

Pinch of Chili Powder

1 T Leaf Thyme

17 oz Canned or Frozen
   Corn

1 C Velveeta Cheese

1 C Evaporated Milk

1 Bottle Clam Juice

1 T Lemon Juice

DIRECTIONS

Dice and boil potatoes, onions and celery in salted water till almost done.

Drain clam juice from clams and save.

Saute clams, red pepper, chili powder, and thyme in butter.

Drain juice from corn if you used canned and save.

Add grated cheese to potato mixture

Add evaporated milk and other juices

Thicken as desired with cornstarch mixture and add lemon juice

"I love clam chowder and this is my favorite recipe!"

Sharon C. G.

Quick Green Chili

- -

INGREDIENTS

1 Large can mushroom soup (can be lowfat)

1 Large can of whole green chilies (sliced thin)

1 Large onion chopped

1 Large green pepper (optional)

1 or 2 Cans Tomatoes and Green Chilies

2 or 3 garlic cloves (or powder)

Cooked chicken chunks

Cumin to taste

Salt and pepper

Chili powder to taste or for hotness (can add jalapenos)

DIRECTIONS

Combine tomatoes and cans of green chilies in a large saucepan. Then add enough water to make chili the consistency you want. Add the rest of the ingredients and simmer until all veggies are thoroughly cooked.

Succotash Soup
Makes 8 to 10 servings

- -

DIRECTIONS

In 5-quart Dutch oven combine and bring to boiling. Reduce heat, cover and simmer for 1-1/2 hours.

1-1/2 lb Corned Beef Brisket

1 Medium Carrot, chopped (1/2 c.)

1 Stalk Celery, chopped (1/2 c.)

8 C Water

Add and simmer, covered, for 45 to 50 minutes or till beef and chicken are tender.

1-1/2 to 3 lb Broiler-fryer Chicken, cut up

Remove beef and chicken; strain broth, discarding, vegetables.* Spoon fat from broth. Cool beef and chicken slightly. Remove and discard skin and bones from chicken. Cut up beef and chicken; set aside. Add, cover and simmer about 20 minutes or until lima beans are almost tender.

2 Medium Potatoes, peeled, chopped (2 c.)

2 C Fresh Lima Beans or 10-oz. Lima Beans, frozen

1 Medium Onion, chopped (1/2 c.)

1/2 tsp Sage, dried, crushed

1/4 tsp Pepper

Cut fresh corn from cobs. Stir fresh or frozen corn, beef, and chicken into soup. Return to boil. Cover and simmer about 15 minutes or till vegetables are tender. Season to taste with salt and pepper.

4 Ears Corn or 10 oz Whole Kernel Corn, frozen

*At this point I refrigerate overnight and finish the next day. It is an excellent soup!

Cindy L., South Charleston

The Best Quick Chili EVER

INGREDIENTS

1 lb Ground Beef or Bison

15.25 oz Can Black Beans

14.5 oz Can Petite Diced Tomatoes, drained (the kind w/sweet onion is preferable)

8 oz Can Tomato Sauce

Maggi Chicken Bouillon Powder

Onion Powder

Garlic Powder

Dried Oregano

Cayenne Pepper Powder

Chili Powder

Cumin

DIRECTIONS

Brown beef/bison in 2 qt saucepan until no longer pink. Drain off grease.

Add black beans, diced tomatoes, and tomato sauce.

Stir, bring to a boil, and reduce to a simmer.

Add herbs and spices to taste. Be careful adding the bouillon - it's very salty. Be generous with the chili powder and cumin - you want it to taste like chili!

Simmer for at least 15 minutes (30 minutes is better).

Salads

Almond Crunch Coleslaw
Bobbie's Frozen Cranberry Salad
Brussels Sprout Salad
Cauliflower Rice Mediterranean Salad
Corn and Bean Salad
Creamy Cole Slaw - Food Processor
Kale Salad with Cranberries
Lemon Quinoa Veggie Salad
Lillian's Chicken Salad
Marshmallow Salad
Mom's Spinach Salad
Pesto Tortellini Salad
Red White & Blue Salad
Strawberry Jell-O Pretzel Salad
Taco Salad
Watermelon Feta Salad

Almond Crunch Coleslaw

- -

INGREDIENTS

1 Bag Grocery Store
  Coleslaw

1 Bunch Green Onions
  (sliced)

1 C Slivered Almonds
  (toasted)

2 Packs Chicken
  Flavored Ramen
  Noodles - (spice packs
  reserved for dressing)

DRESSING INGREDIENTS

3/4 Cup Oil

4 tsp Sugar

1/2 C Apple Cider or
  Rice Vinegar

Spice Packs from
  Ramen Noodles

DIRECTIONS

Crush noodles and combine with slaw,
almonds, and onions.

Combine dressing ingredients, pour over
salad, toss.

Bobbie's Frozen Cranberry Salad
This was a staple at Christmas

- - - - - - - - - - - - - - - - - - - -

INGREDIENTS

8 oz. package of cream cheese

2 T Miracle Whip®

2 T sugar

14 oz. can whole cranberry sauce

8 oz. can crushed pineapple, drained

1 envelope of Dream Whip® (prepared according to directions)

1/2 cup chopped walnuts or pecans

1/2 gallon paper milk carton (cleaned to set in and freeze ingredients)

DIRECTIONS

In a large bowl, with electric mixer, mix cream cheese, pineapple, Miracle Whip®, and sugar.

Fold in cranberries and nuts. Fold in Dream Whip®.

Spoon all ingredients into milk carton and freeze overnight.

Peel away carton and slice (approx. 1.5 inches) or desired thickness.

Serve on lettuce leaves (garnish) on plate.

Kathy L., Akron

Brussels Sprout Salad

INGREDIENTS

1-2 packages of fresh Brussels sprouts or about 4 large handfulls of loose Brussels sprouts.

1 container Blue Cheese or Gorgonzola

3/4 cup dried cranberries

1 cup toasted and chopped walnuts

DRESSING INGREDIENTS

Juice of about 2 lemons

1/2 C Olive Oil

Parmesan cheese, a few shakes

DIRECTIONS

Cut stems off of Brussels sprouts. Slice thin or use a mandolin to slice. Place in a large bowl.

Add Gorgonzola or Blue Cheese, dried cranberries, and chopped walnuts.

Combine all dressing ingredients and stir until thoroughly mixed.

Pour dressing over sprouts & other ingredients. Mix well.

Let salad sit out & stir a bit before serving.

Enjoy!

Cauliflower Rice Mediterranean Salad

- -

For Pot Luck / Party - Servings: 25

SALAD INGREDIENTS:
12 C Cauliflower Riced (Cooked and Cooled)
1 C Pine Nuts, Toasted
1 14 ounce Can, Quartered Artichoke Hearts (Chopped and Drained)
4 C baby Spinach, Roughly Chopped
1 C Red Onion, Chopped
2 C Feta Cheese
2 C Cherry Tomatoes, Halved or Chopped
1 7 ounce Jar Sun-dried Tomatoes in Olive Oil (Chop and add the oil to mixture)

DRESSING INGREDIENTS
2 tsp Sea Salt
1/2 tsp Pepper
1 tsp Dried Basil, Dried Tarragon, or use Fresh Herbs, Chopped (approximately 2 T)
2 Lemons, juiced
1/2 C Olive Oil
2 T Rice Vinegar

Cook the cauliflower rice and then chill for two hours or overnight.

Once chilled, combine all salad ingredients in a bowl and mix.
Combine salad dressing ingredients in a separate bowl and whisk well.
Add the dressing to the salad ingredients and mix well. Serve immediately or chilled.

Tips:
Buy the frozen bags of cauliflower rice. Cook the night before and cool overnight in the refrigerator or microwave to break up and put it in the refrigerator. By the time you prepare the other ingredients, it will be cooled enough to add to the mixture.
You can half or quarter the recipe for smaller gatherings. Leftovers taste great, too!

Extras that can be added:
Kalamata Olives (Drained and rinsed)
Capers (Drained and rinsed)
Garbanzo Beans (Drained and rinsed)

Shelley K., Copley

Corn and Bean Salad

- -

INGREDIENTS

1 C Black Beans, drained
and rinsed

1 C Corn, drained and
rinsed

1 Onion, finely chopped

1 Red Pepper, finely
chopped

3 Chopped Scallions

Dry or fresh Cilantro to
taste (I like a lot)

DRESSING INGREDIENTS

1/4 C Avocado Oil (or
olive or vegetable oil.
Anything mild)

Juice of 1/2 a Lime

1/2 tsp Chili Powder

1 tsp Cumin

Garlic powder, Salt, and
Pepper to taste

DIRECTIONS

Combine all salad ingredients into a bowl and
mix thoroughly.

In a separate bowl, whisk all dressing
ingredients together.

Pour dressing over chopped salad and stir
gently.

Creamy Cole Slaw - Food Processor

DIRECTIONS

Place in food processor with regular blade and whiz until minced:

   1/3 C Parsley Leaves, loosely packed, optional

Add, and whiz until minced:

   2 oz Piece Onion, peeled, sliced

Add and process 5 seconds to combine:

   2/3 C Mayonnaise

   1/3 C Sweetener, your choice

   1 T Red Wine Vinegar

   1/2 tsp Salt

   1/2 tsp Pepper, freshly ground

Insert shredding disc and process:

   1 Large Carrot, peeled, cut in half

   1 Medium Head Green Cabbage, about 2 lbs., core, cut into wedges

Keep an eye on the food processor bowl and empty into a medium serving bowl as needed. Then stir to blend all ingredients.

Serve immediately or refrigerate for up to 24 hours.

Before serving, drain excess liquid and adjust seasoning. Serve chilled.

Cindy L., South Charleston

Kale Salad with Cranberries
Makes 6 servings

DIRECTIONS

Place in a small jar and shake vigorously to mix:

- 1/4 C Lemon Juice, fresh

- 1/4 C Olive Oil

- 2 T Honey or Maple Syrup

- 1 Clove Garlic, minced

- 1/4 tsp Salt

Set aside. Place in a bowl:

1 head of kale, rib removed, very thinly sliced (lacinato/dinosaur or Italian kale preferred)

Add and massage the kale with your hands for a few minutes until the leaves turn darker and wilt slightly:

- 1 - 2 T Lemon Dressing mixture

Add:

- 1/2 C Red Cabbage, chopped or sliced thinly

- 1 Carrot, peeled, grated

- 1 T Red onion finely chopped, optional

- 1/2 C Cranberries, dried

- 1/2 C Feta cheese, optional

- 1/2 C Apple diced

Add:

- 2 T Lemon dressing mixture

Kale Salad with Cranberries (continued)

- -

toss together, taste for seasonings. Top each serving with a bit of:

1/2 C Almonds, slivered, toasted or Sunflower Seeds

Serve and enjoy!

Notes: Can be made up to 3 days in advance, store in an airtight container in the frig. Add the apple and almond right before serving when making in advance. Massaging the kale might sound fancy, but it really is useful just use both hands and rub the dressing into the greens, the kale will wilt and soften slightly making a delicious salad.

Cindy L., South Charleston

Lemon Quinoa Veggie Salad
Makes 4 servings

- -

DIRECTIONS

Place in a large pot and simmer for 15 - 20 minutes, stirring occasionally, until liquid is absorbed and quinoa is cooked:

    4 C Vegetable Broth

    1-1/2 C Quinoa

Add and stir to combine:

    1 C Frozen Mixed Veggies, thawed

Remove from heat, add and combine:

    1/4 C Lemon juice

    1/4 C Olive Oil

    1 Garlic Clove, minced

    1/2 tsp Sea Salt

    1/4 tsp Black Pepper, ground

    2 T Cilantro or Parsley, fresh, chopped, optional

Serve hot or cold.

Lillian's Chicken Salad

INGREDIENTS

3 hard boiled eggs, finely chopped

1 cup celery, finely chopped

1 cup onion, finely chopped

3 tablespoons sweet pickle relish

1 cup elbow macaroni

1 package FROZEN Green Giant Baby Peas (do NOT use CANNED peas)

1 lb. boneless chicken, cooked and finely shredded

Kraft® Real Mayo - 16 oz. jar (do NOT use Hellmann's® !!)

16 oz. bottle creamy French dressing

DIRECTIONS

Mix chopped celery, onion, and egg, and sweet pickle relish together in large mixing bowl.

Cook frozen peas according to package directions, then drain and add to bowl.

Cook elbow macaroni for approximately 12 minutes in boiling water; drain, rinse with cold water and drain, then add to bowl.

Add the chicken after it has been finely shredded.

Mix all ingredients thoroughly.

Add about 2/3 of the jar of mayo and almost half of the bottle of French dressing, and mix thoroughly; add more of mayo and/or French dressing if needed for personal taste preference.

Chill and serve COLD.

Lynn W., Belpre

Marshmallow Salad

INGREDIENTS

I lb can crushed pineapple, drained

I cup mini marshmallows

I pkg instant pistachio pudding mix

I (12 oz) tub Cool Whip®

DIRECTIONS

Mix all ingredients together.

Spread into serving dish or bowl, and refrigerate 24 hours before serving.

Mom's Spinach Salad

INGREDIENTS

1 Head Lettuce

1/3 Pkg Spinach

1/3 C Sugar

1 tsp Salt

1 tsp Dry Mustard

1 tsp Grated Onion

1 (6 oz) Can Cashews

1/4 C Vinegar

1 C Oil

1 tsp Celery Seed

DIRECTIONS

Mix sugar, salt, mustard, onion, and vinegar in 2 cup jar (ex. empty peanut butter jar).

Pour oil slowly in a fine stream into mixture and beat at the same time.

Slowly add celery seed.

Pour dressing over lettuce and spinach. Sprinkle cashews over top of salad.

(May store dressing in the refrigerator).

Pesto Tortellini Salad

INGREDIENTS

1 (20 ounce)
   Refrigerated Tortellini
   - any type

1 C Cherry Tomatoes,
   halved

1 (11 ounce) Jar Kalamata
   Olives, Drained, Rinsed,
   Pitted and Halved

1 (14 ounce) Can
   Artichoke Hearts
   Drained and Roughly-
   chopped.

1 C Feta Cheese,
   Crumbled

1 (7-ounce) Jar Sun-dried
   Tomatoes packed in oil,
   Chopped. Keep the oil
   and add to the pasta

1 (6 ounce) Jar Basil
   Pesto

DIRECTIONS

Cook the tortellini according to package
directions, then drain and rinse with cold
water to stop the cooking process.

Place the pasta in a large bowl and gently
toss to coat with the pesto sauce.

Add in the rest of the ingredients and toss
gently so as not to tear the tortellini. Serve
immediately or chill. If you make ahead,
make sure you mix before serving. Great
for leftovers!

Red White & Blue Salad

INGREDIENTS

2 c. Sliced fresh strawberries

1 pint fresh blueberries

2 c. Heavy whipping cream

4 oz cream cheese, softened

1/2 c. Powdered Erythritol Sweetener (such as swerve)

DIRECTIONS

Pour the heavy whipping cream into a cold glass or metal bowl and beat with electric mixer to thicken slightly.

Add the cream cheese and erythritol Sweetener and continue to beat the mixture until fluffy and slightly firm.

When desired texture is achieved, fold in the strawberries and blueberries.

Can be served immediately, or stored in an airtight container in the refrigerator for up to 2 days.

Serves 4-6

Claudia A., Findlay

Strawberry Jell-O® Pretzel Salad

INGREDIENTS

4 cups pretzels, coarsely chopped

1-1/2 cups melted butter

8 oz cream cheese, soft

2 cups sugar

8 oz Cool Whip®

6 oz strawberry Jell-o®

1 (10 oz) package frozen strawberries

3 tsp sugar

DIRECTIONS

Preheat oven to 400 degrees F.

Mix pretzels, melted butter, and 3 tsp sugar in bowl, then spread into 9x13 pan.

Bake at 400 degrees for 8 minutes. Do not overbake.

In separate bowl, beat cream cheese and 2 cups of sugar together. Fold in Cool Whip®. Spread it over the pretzel mix and refrigerate for 30 minutes.

While in the refrigerator, stir the Jell-o mix into 2 cups of boiling water, then add the strawberries. When the 30 minutes is up, pour it over the cream cheese mixture.

Finally, refrigerate until fully set.

Taco Salad

INGREDIENTS

1 Head Lettuce, Shredded

Green Onions, Chopped

1 Lb. Hamburger

1 Package Taco Seasoning (use two if you want it spicier)

Tomatoes, Chopped

2 C Shredded Sharp Cheddar Cheese

1 large Bottle of 1000 Island Dressing

Crushed Taco Chips

DIRECTIONS

Fry 1 lb. Hamburger, drain grease.

Add taco seasoning.

Mix all ingredients in a very large bowl.

Serve warm or cold with Salsa and extra chips.

"Janice's Tip: I do not give amounts for the onions, tomatoes, and crushed taco chips. Use whatever you like. You can't go wrong. It is also good to add other ingredients such as green peppers, white onions, carrots - doesn't matter as long as you like what goes in. This serves a lot of people, so invite friends over to share."

Janice T., Morrow, Ohio

Watermelon Feta Salad

INGREDIENTS

3 lb Watermelon
  seedless, chilled

8 oz Feta Cheese,
  crumbled

3/4 C Fresh Basil,
  chopped

DRESSING INGREDIENTS

1/3 C Extra Virgin Olive
  Oil

2 Limes, juiced

1 - 1/2 tsp Salt

1 tsp Fresh Ground
  Black Pepper

DIRECTIONS

Cut out rind from watermelon. Chop the fruit into 1 inch cubes.

In a small bowl whisk together olive oil, lime juice, salt, and pepper.

In a large bowl combine watermelon cubes, crumbled feta and basil leaves. Toss gently until ingredients are combined well. Transfer to serving bowl. Sprinkle few basil leaves on top.

Drizzle the dressing over the salad. Stir gently to integrate the cheese and dressing into the salad.

Serve chilled.

Side Dishes

Corn Souffle

Kale and Sweet Potato Hash

Mom's Famous Sweet Potato Casserole

Reunion Baked Beans

Scalloped Potatoes

Simple Sautéed Kale

Corn Souffle

INGREDIENTS

1 can whole kernel corn, drained

1 can creamed corn

1 box Jiffy corn muffin mix

2 eggs

1 cup sour cream

3/4 stick of butter, melted

DIRECTIONS

Preheat oven to 350 degrees F, and grease 9x13 baking dish.

Mix all ingredients together.

Pour into greased dish.

Bake for 45-50 minutes or until set and lightly brown on top.

Kale and Sweet Potato Hash

INGREDIENTS

1 Bunch Kale of Choice (3-4 cups

1-2 Large Sweet Potatoes, cooked and diced (Speedy substitute suggestion: replace with a can of yams or red potatoes. When substituting red potatoes, I'll add a can of cooked carrots for color and nutritional content.)

1-2 Beyond Meat sausage Links, thawed (Optional; could swap for a meat/meat substitute of choice)

1 T Extra Virgin Olive Oil (optional substitution: coconut oil)

1 T Maple Syrup

1/2 T Cumin

2 tsp Garlic Powder (or 1 garlic clove, minced)

2 tsp Onion Powder

A Dash of Smoked Paprika

Sea salt and Freshly Ground Pepper, to taste

Optional: Nutritional Yeast

*All spices are approximate amounts. Feel free to add more or less according to your preference.

DIRECTIONS

In a large bowl, prepare kale to be sautéed. Remove leaves from stems and tear into pieces. Drizzle with olive oil, sprinkle with salt and freshly ground pepper, and massage for 2-3 minutes with your hands, coating and softening the kale. Transfer to a large skillet and saute with olive oil until kale has wilted. Allow some of the kale to crisp for added texture and taste.

Meanwhile, dice up Beyond Meat sausage links into 1/2 inch chunks and add to the skillet. Allow to brown evenly, approximately 4-5 minutes. Add the sweet potatoes to the skillet as well, along with the spices and maple syrup. Stir to coat, adding more salt and pepper to taste.
Cook an additional 2-3 minutes, allowing flavors to mingle and all ingredients to warm through.

This dish has been adapted many times in my kitchen and is a great dish to serve as a side in cooler Autumn months.

Sarah D., Summit County

Mom's Famous Sweet Potato Casserole

INGREDIENTS

1 (29 oz) and 1 (40 oz) cans yams, mashed

1 cup sugar

1/2 tsp salt

2 eggs, slightly beaten

1/3 stick butter, melted

1/2 cup milk

1 tsp vanilla

STREUSEL TOPPING INGREDIENTS

1 cup brown sugar

1/2 cup flour

1 cup chopped walnuts

1/3 stick butter, soft

DIRECTIONS

Preheat oven to 350 degrees F.

Mix all casserole ingredients together.

Pour into greased dish.

To make the streusel topping, mix together the brown sugar, flour, and walnuts. Add the butter last.

Spoon the topping all over the yam mixture, and bake for 50-60 minutes until set.

Reunion Baked Beans

INGREDIENTS

1 Lb Ground Beef

1 Large Sweet Onion

3/4 Lb Bacon, cooked and chopped

4-15 oz Can Pork and Beans

1-18 oz Bottle Honey BBQ Sauce

1-16 oz Can Kidney Beans (drain & rinse)

1-15 oz Can Butter Beans (drain & rinse)

1-15 oz Can Black Beans (drain & rinse)

1/4 C Brown Sugar

1/4 C Molasses

3 T Vinegar

1 tsp Salt

1/2 tsp Pepper

DIRECTIONS

Preheat the oven to 350° F.

In a large skillet cook beef and onions over medium heat until meat is no longer pink; drain.

Transfer meat to a 5-qt Dutch oven. Stir in the remaining ingredients.

Cover and Bake at 350 degrees for 1 hour.

If you are not ready to serve, place in a Crockpot on warm, do not overcook by using low or high on the crock pot.

Leftovers can be refrigerated but should be warmed up preferably in a microwave or saucepan, not crock pot or oven.

Serves 18

Barbara H., Uniontown

Scalloped Potatoes

DIRECTIONS

Mix Together:

      6 T Flour (Cornstarch may be used for gluten-free recipes)

      4 C Cold Milk

Slice 5 pounds of potatoes.

Alternate salt, milk/flour mixture, potatoes; put extra milk on top and top with 1 stick of butter.

Bake at 325 F for 2.5 hours

Simple Sautéed Kale

INGREDIENTS

Olive oil

Kale (any variety or a mixture)

Garlic (fresh cloves or dehydrated powder or granules)

Sea salt

Pepper (freshly ground is best)

DIRECTIONS

Heat a large cast-iron pan on low. Add olive oil to coat the bottom well and let it heat up gently.

Strip kale leaves from the spine and chop or tear into 2-3 inch pieces. Wash them well (I use a salad spinner).

Turn heat under pan to medium. Add kale leaves and stir them continuously while they cook.

Add salt, pepper, and garlic to taste.

Do not add garlic too early, as it cooks more quickly than kale and can burn if added too early. Add a couple tablespoons of water to sauté pain if needed to help kale leaves get soft.

Serve as a side dish or as base for other foods such as meat, potatoes, or other vegetables.

Janet L., Lakewood

Main Dishes

Chicken Parisienne
Chicken Slop
Crock Pot Swedish Meatballs
Deli Wraps
Easy Taco Rice Casserole
Easy Weeknight Quiche
Everyone's Favorite Fried Chicken!
Fettuccine Alfredo Vegan Style and Delicious!
Fiesta Chicken
Grandma Esta's Meat Ravioli
Leftover Taco Meat Recipes
Magic Quiche
Ma's Special Burritos
No Crust Salmon Quiche
Palmini® Lasagne
Pepper Steak
Pierogi Casserole
Pulled BBQ
Rice and Tuna Pie
Shredded Chicken in Crock Pot
Simply Old Fashioned and Easy Stuffed Cabbage
Six-Layer Dish
Sloppy Joes
Spicy Liberty Chicken Sandwiches
Spicy Porcupine Meatballs
Swedish Meatballs
Swiss Chicken
Taco Casserole
Turkey Enchiladas

Chicken Parisienne

- -

DIRECTIONS

Preheat oven to 350 degrees F

Place 4 large or medium chicken breasts, skin side up, in 11x7x1-1/2 inch baking dish.

Combine 1 can condensed cream of mushroom soup, a 3 ounce can (2/3 cup) mushrooms and liquid, 1 cup sour cream, and 1/2 cup cooking sherry. Pour over chicken.

Sprinkle generously with paprika.

Bake for 1 to 1-1/4 hours or until tender.

Serve with hot fluffy rice.

Lisa M., Streetsboro

Chicken Slop

- - - - - - - - - - - - - - - - - - - -

INGREDIENTS

2 Cans of Cream of
  Celery Soup (the non
  heart healthy works
  best)

1 16oz Tub of Sour
  Cream

1 Pkg of Boneless
  Skinless Chicken
  Breast

DIRECTIONS

Mix soup and sour cream together well.
Cut chicken into bite size chunks; add to
soup mixture.

Put in a slow cooker on high for an hour
or until chicken is done. Stir occasionally.
Serve over cooked white rice.

"I don't have a name for this
dish other than what I have
always called it for my kids,
"Chicken Slop", which doesn't
sound at all appetizing. It's a
take on chicken Parisian"

Crock Pot Swedish Meatballs

INGREDIENTS

2 (10 oz) cans Cream of
   Mushroom soup

16 oz sour cream

24 oz beef broth

2 tsp celery salt

2 tsp smoked paprika

2 tsp garlic powder

2 Tbsp fresh or dried
   parsley

Black pepper to taste

2 Tbsp Worcestshire

2 lbs frozen turkey
   meatballs

Egg noodle

DIRECTIONS

Put all except egg noodles in crock pot.

Set on LOW for 4 hours, but switch to
HIGH for last 30 minutes.

Serve over cooked egg noodles.

Courtney K.

Deli Wraps

INGREDIENTS

2 blocks cream cheese

small container sour
    cream

2 T ranch dip mix

2 cups chopped spinach

3 mini bell peppers,
    chopped

2 stalks celery

1 package turkey bacon,
    chopped

cranberries to taste

flour tortillas

DIRECTIONS

Mix all ingredients well.

Layer tortilla, lettuce, then lunch meat.. Add
roughly, 2 tablespoons of the mix to the
outer edge and roll.

Easy Taco Rice Casserole

INGREDIENTS

4 C of uncooked rice

4 Pounds of Hamburger

2 16 oz. Bottles of Taco Sauce

4 1 oz. Packages of Taco Seasoning

1/2-3/4 C of Water

1 3.5 oz. Can of Sliced Black Olives

1/4 C Chopped Red Onion

3-4 C of Shredded Cheddar or Mexican Blend Cheese

8-12 oz. of Sour Cream

3.5-4 oz. Bag of Tortilla Strips

DIRECTIONS

Cook the rice and stir in one 16 oz bottle of taco sauce. Cook and drain the hamburger then mix in the taco seasoning with 1/2-3/4 cups of water. Stir until the seasoning is well blended with the hamburger.

Evenly spread rice into a 13" x 18" inch, (1/2 sheet cake), pan. Spoon and spread the hamburger over the rice.

Sprinkle the olives and red onions evenly over the top of the meat and rice. Liberally layer the shredded cheese over the top of the casserole.

Loosely cover and slightly tent the pan with aluminum foil and heat at 400 degrees F for about 20 minutes, or until the cheese is well melted. Garnish each serving with a dollop of sour cream, a small handful of tortilla strips, and a good sized drizzle of taco sauce.

Jenny N., Canton

Easy Weeknight Quiche

- -

INGREDIENTS

2 C Milk (2%)

4 Large Eggs

3/4 C Bisquick®

1/2 Stick Unsalted Butter

1 C Shredded Parmesan

1/2 C Diced Ham (the type on the lunch-meat aisle)

4 oz Shredded Sharp Cheddar

2 C Fresh Baby Spinach Leaves

Onion Powder

Garlic Powder

Salt

Pepper

Coconut oil

DIRECTIONS

Preheat oven to 375 degrees F.

Mix milk, eggs, and Bisquick® in a big bowl. It will be slightly lumpy.

Melt butter in microwave at 50% power. Add to bowl.

Add Parmesan, ham, and cheddar.

Tear tough stems off spinach leaves and discard. Tear leaves into small pieces and add to bowl.

Add dashes of onion powder, garlic powder, salt, and pepper. Mix.

Grease a 10" glass pie plate with coconut oil, and pour everything in.

Bake for 50 minutes.

Let sit for about 10 minutes before slicing.

Everyone's Favorite Fried Chicken!

INGREDIENTS

4 to 6 breasts of
  organic boneless
  chicken - Rinse
  and clean properly
  (butterfly it if you like
  a lot of breading!)

One cup of whole wheat
  or white flour

One cup of whole
  uncooked oats

One cup of seasoned
  breadcrumbs

2 cups of organic milk

3 to 4 cups of canola or
  regular cooking oil

Garlic salt to taste

DIRECTIONS

Mix all dry ingredients in a bowl and set
aside. Put the milk in a bowl and set aside.
Drench the chicken breasts in the milk then
into the dry mixture. Cover it thoroughly!

Slowly place each chicken breast into the
frying pan with approximately 2 inches of
cooking oil over medium heat. Do not put
the chicken in until the oil is heated. Allow
the chicken to cook for approximately five
minutes on each side. Be sure it is browned
before you turn it. Season the chicken with
garlic salt. (Not garlic seasoning!)

After each chicken breast is done cooking, place in a large glass dish. Pour the
excess oil over the chicken and cook in the
oven for an additional 35 minutes at 375°F
Uncovered. If you cover the chicken it will
become soggy. It's better crispy!

I use the excess cooking oil to pour over
my animals dry food for the next few
days.

Mary Frances W., Rocky River

Fettuccine Alfredo Vegan Style and Delicious!

INGREDIENTS

1/2 C Raw Cashews

2 T Nutritional Yeast

1 tsp Cornstarch

1/2 tsp Onion Granules or Powder

1/2 tsp Salt

1/8 tsp Black or White Pepper

2 Medium Cloves of Garlic

1-1/4 C Water

DIRECTIONS

Allow cashews to soak in the water for a few hours in a blender or VitaMix.

Add all other ingredients and blend thoroughly.

Pour into a sauce pan and stir constantly over med/high heat until thick and bubbly, then remove from heat (do not walk away while cooking, otherwise you will scorch and make lumpy).

Pour over cooked fettuccine, then add freshly chopped parsley, and vegan Parmesan cheese.

Will serve 3 using 1lb box of fettuccine. Double recipe for 6.

Serve with steamed broccoli or roasted Brussels sprouts.

Fiesta Chicken

INGREDIENTS

1-1/2 - 2 Pounds of
   Boneless Skinless
   Chicken Breast

1 Can of Corn, Drained

2 C of Salsa

1 Can Black Beans,
   Drained and Rinsed

8oz Cream Cheese,
   Cubed

DIRECTIONS

Place first four ingredients into crock-pot.
Cook on low for 3-4 hours.

Shred the chicken. Add cream cheese on
top and cook another 30 minutes. Stir
together.

Can serve over rice (our favorite), with
tortilla chips, or rolled into a burrito.

"One of our family's fav
recipes. It's loved by all of us!"

Shawna S., Athens County

Grandma Esta's Meat Ravioli

DOUGH INGREDIENTS

4 C Flour

4 Eggs

1 tsp Oil

1 tsp Salt

Water as needed

FILLING INGREDIENTS

1 lb Ground Veal & Pork

1/4 Clove Garlic
(Use more if you like)

1 C Bread crumbs

1 Small Onion

2 T Chopped Parsley

2 Eggs

1/4 C Parmesan Cheese
(Use more if you like)

Salt & pepper to taste

DIRECTIONS

Mix flour, salt on floured board. Work eggs well into flour. Add only enough water to make a stiff dough. Add oil with the water. Knead until smooth.

Place a bowl over dough, let rest for 1/2 hour.

Make filling: Brown meat in oil then cool. Place in bowl with rest of ingredients and blend well. Taste, may need more salt, pepper, cheese, or garlic. Then use garlic powder.

Cut a small piece of dough & roll out in a noodle machine or by hand. Dough is rolled out long enough to fold over the plate.

Place a layer of rolled dough over ravioli plate, place small balls of meat filling in each square then cover with another layer of dough. Fill the squares over dough on plate.

Can freeze. I layer plates on floured wax paper. That way can cook a few plates at time.

Wrap good will foil then put in bags.

Use your favorite sauce.

Variations:

Spinach and cheese ravioli.

Ground chicken, turkey, or beef with the pork & veal.

Leftover Taco Meat Recipes

Taco Omelette:

-Mix leftover taco meat with scrambled eggs, cook

-Add cheddar cheese or Colby jack before folding eggs over in pan

-Top with salsa before serving

Taco Pizza:

Using a flatbread, bagel, English muffin, or pizza crust, sauce your base with salsa or taco sauce. Add the leftover taco meat, top with cheddar or Colby jack cheese, and bake in the oven at 350 F degrees until the cheese is melted (usually about 10 minutes).

Tanya R., Parma

Magic Quiche

INGREDIENTS

1 C Shredded Swiss or Cheddar Cheese

4-5 Eggs

2 C Milk or Cream

1/2 C Whole Wheat Flour or Baking Mix

1/2 cup cooked meat (bacon/ham/sausage etc)

1/2 cup chopped raw veggie (peppers/onions/ mushrooms etc)

Salt and pepper to Taste

DIRECTIONS

Layer the meat, cheese, veggie into a buttered 8-9in pie dish.

In a separate bowl beat the eggs, milk, flour, spices

Pour egg mixture over the pie dish/other ingredients LET SIT FOR 5 minutes

Oven: Bake 350° F for 50-60 minutes.

Ma's Special Burritos

INGREDIENTS

1 - 8oz Pkg Cream Cheese

1/2 C Salsa

1/2 C Shredded Mexican Blend or Cheddar Cheese

15 Black Olives

4-6 10-inch Flour Tortillas

DIRECTIONS

1) Mix cream cheese and salsa. I use a large spoon.

2) Blend in shredded cheese and olives.

3) Place in tortillas and wrap like a burrito.

4) Serve and enjoy!

Duane & Sally J.

No Crust Salmon Quiche

INGREDIENTS

3 Eggs

1/2 C Biscuit or Pancake Mix

6 T Melted butter (3/4 of stick)

1-1/4 C Milk (2%)

1/4 tsp Salt, Pepper, and Garlic Powder

1/2 C Sharp Cheddar, cubed small

1/2 C Sharp Cheddar shredded, (for top)

1-1/2 C Salmon (or Ham or Turkey)

1 C Mixed Vegetables (peas, carrots, green beans or whatever)

DIRECTIONS

Place all ingredients except cheese and meat into blender and mix.

Pour into greased 9-inch pan.

Put Veggies, cubed cheese and meat into pan and toss.

Pour mixture over top.

Top with shredded cheese.

Pat down with fork.

Top with Paprika (optional)

BAKE AT 350 degrees F for 50 to 55 minutes. Test with knife in center.

Cool 10 minutes and serve.

ENJOY!

"This recipe is over 40 years old and comes from an Alaskan fisherman's wife.
It can also be made with ham or turkey instead of salmon."

Palmini® Lasagne

INGREDIENTS

8 oz. 80/20 grass fed ground beef

1/2 c. Ricotta cheese

1/4 tsp salt

Dash black pepper

1/4 tsp garlic salt

1/4 tsp Italian seasoning

2 c. Yo Mama's brand basil pasta sauce

1 can Palmini® Lasagne sheets

7 slices mozzarella cheese

1/2 can sliced mushrooms

1/4 c. Parmesan cheese

DIRECTIONS

Preheat oven to 350°F

Spray sides and bottom of a standard bread loaf pan with non-stick cooking oil, set aside.

In a greased skillet, cook the 8 oz beef until browned, drain excess grease. To the beef, add the 2 c pasta sauce and mushrooms, bring to a simmer then remove from heat.

In a separate bowl, mix the ricotta, Parmesan, salt, pepper, garlic salt and Italian seasoning until well combined. Set aside.

Drain and rinse Palmini® Lasagne sheets thoroughly. Line the bottom of the loaf pan with one layer of Palmini® sheets (it took 5 to do each layer for my loaf pan, but this can vary). Drop and spread an even layer of the beef mixture on top of the Palmini®i layer, top this layer with 2 slices of mozzarella cheese.

Place the next layer of Palmini® noodles, Drop and spread an even layer of the beef mixture on top of the Palmini® layer, top this with the ricotta mixture, spread evenly, top with 2 slices of mozzarella cheese.

Place the final layer of Palmini® noodles, Drop and spread an even layer of the beef mixture on top of the Palmini® layer and top with remaining cheese slices.

Cover with foil and bake in Preheated oven for 30 minutes. Remove foil and continue to bake an additional 15 minutes. Let stand 10 minutes before cutting/serving.

Makes 4-6 servings

Claudia A., Findlay

Pepper Steak

INGREDIENTS

1.5 lbs Round Steak

1/4 C Flour

1/2 tsp Salt

1/8 tsp Pepper

1/4 C Olive Oil

8oz Can Tomatoes

1 3/4 C Water

1/2 C Chopped Onions

1 T Gravy Master®

2 Green Peppers (cut in strips)

2 C cooked rice

DIRECTIONS

Cut steak into strips.

Combine flour, salt and pepper.

Cook meat in hot oil until browned. Drain tomatoes, reserving the liquid. Add tomato liquid to water, onions, and Gravy Master® to meat.

Cover and simmer for 2 hours until meat is tender. Add green peppers. Cover and simmer for 5 minutes. Add drained tomatoes and cook for 5 minutes.

Serve over hot rice.

Pierogi Casserole

INGREDIENTS

8-10 Potatoes, peeled and cooked

1 lb Shredded Cheddar Cheese

2 Large Diced Onions

9-12 Lasagna Noodles, cooked as directed

2 Sticks of Butter

Salt and Pepper to taste

DIRECTIONS

Preheat the oven to 350 degrees F.

Mash potatoes with cheese.

In a skillet, saute onions in butter until tips are a little brown.

Add half of the onions to the potato mixture. Stir.

Add salt and pepper to taste.

Butter a 13x9 inch baking dish.

Place one layer of noodles in the baking dish, then add a layer of potato mixture. Repeat layers, ending with a layer of noodles.

Pour remaining onion mixture over top.

Cover with foil and Bake for 15 minutes.

Kathy L., Akron

Pulled BBQ

- -

INGREDIENTS

2 LB Beef Roast

1 LB Pork Roast

Salt & Pepper to taste

DIRECTIONS

Place roasts in the oven at 250 degrees F for 3-4 hours. Shred meat when cool then add:

1 Stalk Chopped Celery

1 T Flour

1 Small Bottle Catsup

1 Bottle Water

1 Bottle Chili Sauce

1/4 Bottle Steak Sauce

1/2 C Brown Sugar

Cook 2 hours at 350 degrees F, stirring occasionally. Pull apart with fork when done.

Serve on hamburger buns.

Rice and Tuna Pie
Makes 6 servings

- -

DIRECTIONS

Grease a 9" x 12" baking dish. In large bowl combine, then press onto bottom and sides of prepared dish:

> 2 Eggs, beaten
>
> 4 T Butter, melted
>
> 2 T Onion, chopped (2 t. onion powder)
>
> 1/2 tsp Marjoram, crushed

Add:

> 4 C Brown Rice, cooked and cooled, (short grain preferred)

Place atop:

> 18 oz Canned Tuna, drained and flaked

Reuse that bowl and now combine, then pour over tuna:

> 6 Eggs, beaten
>
> 1-1/2 C Milk
>
> 2 T Onion, chopped (2 t. onion powder)
>
> 1/2 tsp Salt
>
> 1/2 tsp Marjoram, crushed
>
> Dash of pepper

Add:

> 2 C (8 oz.) Swiss cheese, shredded

Bake, uncovered, at 350 degrees till a knife inserted just off-center comes out clean 45 - 50 minutes. If desired garnish with:

> Pimiento, chopped & Parsley, snipped

Cindy L., South Charleston

Shredded Chicken in Crock Pot

- -

INGREDIENTS

3-4 Chicken Breasts, with fat removed

2 Small Cans of Cream of Chicken Soup (or 1 large)

Onion Salt

Garlic Salt

Chicken Bouillon (optional)

Saltine Crackers (2 big packs)

DIRECTIONS

Put chicken, spices, and cream of chicken soup into crock pot. You can add some water (1/2 of a small empty can or 1/4 of a large empty can).

Stir, then cook 6-8 hours on low.
When finished, you can turn off or keep on warm.

You can remove the chicken and cut into pieces, then put back in crock pot.

(I tend to use a meat/potato masher as the chicken is very tender and falls apart.)

Then, add two packs of saltine crackers - this thickens the shredded chicken.
It tastes best fresh, but you can put in the refrigerator for a few days or freeze what you don't eat.

Enjoy!

Simply Old Fashioned and Easy Stuffed Cabbage

INGREDIENTS

Should make 10-12 cabbage rolls!

1-2 heads of Green Cabbage, washed. You can wash the head and take out the core. It's easiest if you pull off the leaves initially. (But save the center to chop up and put in the tomato mixture!)

2 Pounds of Ground Beef. I use 80/20 it's a little more fatty and has better flavor

1 C White Rice, uncooked

2 Small Cans of Tomato Paste

1 Large Can of Diced or Chopped Tomatoes

Salt and Pepper (1/2 teaspoon)

2 Cans of Campbell's Tomato Soup (my secret ingredient!)

1/4 C of Chopped Onions (if desired)

DIRECTIONS

Mix the ground beef with the uncooked white rice. Add onions and half a teaspoon of salt and pepper. Mix with your hands or in your mixer thoroughly.

Take approximately 1/4 cup (or half handful) of the beef and rice mixture and place it on the edge of the uncooked cabbage leaf. Roll like a burrito. Please each individual cabbage roll in a glass pan. Line them up together but not too tight.

Mix all of your canned tomato ingredients together with a mixer. Add 1 to 2 cups of water to the mixture. Add chopped leftover cabbage to the tomato mixture. Pour evenly over the cabbages.

Seal tightly with aluminum foil. Place on a cookie sheet if you are concerned about boiling over.

Cook at 300° F for 4 hours.

"Serve with bread and butter or homemade garlic bread!"

Mary Frances W., Rocky River

Six-Layer Dish
Makes 6 servings

- -

DIRECTIONS

Preheat oven to 300°F.

Layer in order given in a 2 qt.(9"x13") greased casserole:

> 2 Potatoes, medium, sliced
>
> 2 Carrots, medium, sliced
>
> 1/3 C Rice, uncooked
>
> 2 Onions, small, sliced
>
> 1 lb Beef, ground
>
> 1 qt Tomatoes, canned

Sprinkle over with:

> 1 T Brown Sugar

Bake for 2-1/2 - 3 hours.

Options: Just before ground beef add 1 c. cooked kidney beans, drained.

Substitute browned pork sausage for ground beef.

Sloppy Joes

INGREDIENTS

"Honestly I never measure. I just add ingredients until I get the taste I want."

1 Lb. Lean Ground Beef

1 Onion, diced

1 Clove Garlic, minced

1/2 C Ketchup (more or less to taste)

1 C Salsa (more or less to taste)

1 T Mustard (I use the spicy kind and add more if needed)

2-3 Capfuls Cider Vinegar

1 tsp Sugar

DIRECTIONS

Brown meat and onions in large skillet.

Drain off fat.

Add all other ingredients.

Simmer 20-30 minutes.

Janice T., Morrow, Ohio

Spicy Liberty Chicken Sandwiches
(in the air fryer)

- -

Chicken Prep

5-6 Chicken Breasts

1/2 T Paprika

1/4 T Onion Powder

1/2 T Garlic Powder

1/2 T Cajun Seasoning

1/4 T White or Black Pepper

1/4 T Baking Powder (optional)

Place 5-6 chicken breasts in a bowl or on a cutting board (cut off any fat). Mix the above ingredients into the bowl or into a shaker, coating both sides of the chicken. Set the air fryer to 360°F for 26-30 minutes (until proper internal temp is reached). After two minutes into cooking, spray the top of the chicken with cooking spray (optional). Halfway through the cooking process, flip the chicken and spray with cooking spray again (optional).

Spicy Liberty Sauce

1/2 C Mayo

1/2 T Cayenne Pepper

1 Package Hamburger Buns

Butter

Sliced Pickles

Mix mayo and cayenne pepper to taste (depending how hot you like it). Butter your bread/buns and place them in a pan on medium heat to give them a little crisp. Spread the spicy sauce on the bottom bun and add a layer of sliced pickles. When the chicken is done, place it on top of the dressed bun followed by the top bun. Freedom! :)

Spicy Porcupine Meatballs
(in the instant-pot)

- - - - - - - - - - - - - - - - - - - -

MEATBALL INGREDIENTS

1/2 lb Ground Beef

1/2 lb Spicy Sausage
(remove casing)

1 tsp Onion Powder

1/2 tsp Garlic Powder

1/2 tsp Salt

1/2 tsp Black Pepper

1/4 tsp Cayenne

1/4 tsp Crushed Red
Pepper Flakes

1/2 tsp Parsley

4 oz Mozzarella
(shredded or diced)

1/2 C Orzo Pasta

1 Egg

SAUCE INGREDIENTS

1/3 C White Wine
(optional)

1 C Water or Broth

12 oz your favorite
pasta sauce

Parmesan cheese to
top

DIRECTIONS

Mix the meatball ingredients in a mixing bowl.

Form the mixture into golf-ball-sized spheres and place inside your instant-pot.

Pour the wine and water around the meatballs in the instant-pot.

Pour the pasta sauce on top of the meatballs.

Pressure-cook on high for 4 minutes and slow-release for 5-10 minutes. Fully release the pressure manually, remove the lid, and add mozzarella and Parmesan to taste.

Joshua, a Libertarian from Fremont

Swedish Meatballs

- - - - - - - - - - - - - - - - - - -

INGREDIENTS

1 lb Ground Turkey or Beef

1/2 C Chopped Onion

4 Crackers or 1/4 C Bread Crumbs

1 Egg

1 tsp Parsley

1/2 tsp Salt

1/4 tsp Garlic Powder

1/4 tsp Onion Powder

1/4 tsp Paprika

2 T Oil

2 T. Parmesan Cheese

1/4 C Sour Cream or Mayonnaise

DIRECTIONS

Heat oven at 350 degrees F. Grease baking dish. Mix and form into meatballs. Cook 55 minutes or until done.

"I make 3 lbs. at a time and freeze meatballs to eat with spaghetti or mash potatoes and gravy."

Swiss Chicken

INGREDIENTS

8-9 chicken cutlets

4 long slices Swiss
cheese

1-2 cans Cream of
Chicken soup

1/2 cup milk

Plain bread crumbs
1 stick butter, melted

DIRECTIONS

Preheat oven to 350 degrees F, 325 for
glass pan.

Lay cutlets in 9x13 pan. Place Swiss cheese
across top.

Whisk soup and milk together, and pour
over top of chicken.

Sprinkle plain bread crumbs on top, then
drizzle melted better on top of the crumbs.

Bake for 45-50 minutes.

Courtney K.

Taco Casserole

INGREDIENTS

1/2 Bag Tortilla Chips

1 Can Refried Beans

1 lb Ground Beef

1 Packet Taco Seasoning

1 Can Diced Tomatoes

1 Bag Shredded Cheddar Cheese

Optional Ingredients: guacamole, sour cream, shredded lettuce, sliced black olives, jalapenos, diced tomatoes

DIRECTIONS

Place tortilla chips in a large baggie that zips and crush them. Place the crushed chips in the bottom of a 9X13 pan. Spread refried beans on top of crushed chips.

Cook meat with taco seasoning. Once meat is cooked, add the can of diced tomatoes. Pour meat mixture over the refried beans layer. Top with shredded cheese. Bake in the oven at 350 F for 20-25 minutes or until the cheese is melted.

Serve with your favorite taco toppings.

Turkey Enchiladas

INGREDIENTS

2 lbs lean ground turkey

1 small onion, chopped

1 tsp organic taco seasoning

1/2 tsp ground cumin

1/4 tsp pepper

1 (8 oz) cream cheese, cubed

1 cup shredded Mexican cheese

1 can black beans, rinsed and drained

1-1/2 cup frozen corn

1 can fire-roasted tomatoes, drained

1 can chopped green chilis, 2 if you want it spicy

1/4 cup salsa

Tortillas

2 cans enchilada sauce

DIRECTIONS

Preheat oven to 325 degrees F and grease two 9x13 pans.

Cook turkey, onion, and seasonings in Dutch oven until turkey is no longer pink.

Stir in cream cheese and 1/2 cup Mexican cheese.

Stir in beans, corn, tomatoes, chilis, and salsa.

Spoon 1/3 cup mixture on tortilla, roll it up, and lay it seam-side down in pan. Repeat to fill both pans across.

Top each set of enchiladas with the enchilada sauce, and sprinkle the remaining shredded cheese on top.

Bake for 15-20 minutes to melt the cheese.

Courtney K.

Desserts

Aggression Cookies
Apple Cake
Applesauce Cake
Authentic Polish Kolacky
Baclava
Bobbie's Strawberry Shaped Cookies
Caramel Lasagna Dessert
Crepes & Strawberry Puree
Dumped Angel Food Cake
Grandma's Aggression Cookies
Grandma Bean's Apple Dumplings
Grandma's Chocolate Dessert
Grandma's Devil's Food Chocolate Chip Bundt Cake
Mom's Soft Oatmeal Cookies
My Mom's Lemon Cheese Dainties
No Bake Oreo Cake
Nut Milk Chia Seed Pudding
Peanut Butter Buckeyes
Peanut Butter Chocolate Chip Bars
Pumpkin Tea Cake
Pumpkin Wonder Cookies
Red, White, and Blue Trifle
Rhubarb Custard Cake
Rolled Butter Cookies
Secret Family Recipe Chocolate Chip Cookies
S'mores Bars
Strawberry Rhubarb Baked Oatmeal
These cookies are going to be huuuge!

Aggression Cookies

- -

INGREDIENTS

3 C Salted Butter, softened

3 C Flour

3 C Packed Brown Sugar

6 C Oats

1 T Baking Soda

DIRECTIONS

Combine all ingredients in big bowl and mix well with hands just like kneading dough (to get your aggression out).

Roll into balls and bake on ungreased cookie sheet for 10 minutes at 350 degrees F.

Lisa M., Streetsboro

Apple Cake

INGREDIENTS

3 Eggs

1-3/4 C Sugar

1 C Oil

2 C Flour

1 tsp Cinnamon

1 tsp Baking Soda

1/4 tsp Salt

5 Cooking Apples, Cubed

1/2 C Raisins or Nuts

1 tsp Vanilla

DIRECTIONS

Beat eggs and sugar for 5 minutes.

Add oil and dry ingredients.

Add apples and raisins/nuts and beat with wooden spoon until blended.

Bake at 350 F for one hour in an 8x10 oblong pan or large oblong pan.

Applesauce Cake

INGREDIENTS

1-1/4 C All Purpose Four

1/2 tsp Allspice

1/2 tsp Salt

1/2 C Butter

1 tsp Baking Powder

3/4 C Brown Sugar

1 tsp Baking Soda

1 Egg

1 tsp Nutmeg

1 C Applesauce

1 tsp Cinnamon

1 C Raisins

DIRECTIONS

Reserve 1 tablespoon flour to coat raisins.

Mix all dry ingredients together.

Cream the butter; gradually add brown sugar and cream well until light and fluffy.

Add egg and beat well. Add the dry ingredients alternately with the applesauce, a little at a time, beating after each addition ONLY until smooth.

Fold in the floured raisins.

Bake in a greased and lined or floured 8" square pan in a moderate oven (350°F) for 40 to 50 minutes.

Cool 10 minutes before removing from the pan.

Sprinkle with confectioners sugar when cool.

The recipe may be doubled. Refrain from over beating the cake mixture because you want the crumb to be a little coarse. Cake may be iced if desired but plain cake tastes just as good.

"Here is one of my favorite recipes and it's perfect for Ohio since Johnny Appleseed traveled through the area where I lived as a child which was Mansfield Ohio."

Carol C. S., Richmond VA

Authentic Polish Kolacky

INGREDIENTS

8oz Cream Cheese

2 1/2 Sticks of Oleo or Butter

2 1/2 C Sifted Flour

Filling of your choice (i.e., raspberry preserves, apricot preserves, etc.)

DIRECTIONS

Combine first 3 ingredients.

Divide dough in half and chill.

Roll out 1/2 at a time, thin.

Cut in diamond shapes and place filling in the center. Bring ends together.

Bake on ungreased cookie sheet at 350 F for 20 minutes.

Baclava (Courtesy of Gerry Moss)

INGREDIENTS

16 oz. frozen phyllo
   dough (will use all)

1 C butter

2 C walnuts, finely
   chopped

1-1/2 C pecans

2-1/2 C sugar

2 T honey

2 T lemon juice

2" stick cinnamon

3/4 tsp. cinnamon

DIRECTIONS

Thaw phyllo dough at room temperature for 2 hours. Unwrap and cover with slightly damp cloth towel.

Mix walnuts, pecans, 1/2 C sugar, and 3/4 tsp. cinnamon.

Meanwhile in saucepan, combine 2 C sugar, 1 C water, 2 Tbsp. honey, 2 Tbsp. lemon juice, 2 inches stick cinnamon. Boil gently uncovered for 15 minutes. Remove from heat; remove cinnamon. Stir until blended.

Melt butter and lightly butter bottom of 13X9X2 baking pan.

Layer nine sheets in the pan, brush / dab each sheet with some of the butter. Top with four more sheets, brushing each with more of the melted butter. Sprinkle with nuts. Repeat the nut and phyllo sheet layers five more times (total 6 sets of 4 sheets). Sprinkle with remaining nut mixture. Drizzle with some of the melted butter. Top with remaining nine sheets of phyllo, brushing each with some of the remaining butter.

Cut into diamond shaped pieces or squares, but not through to the bottom layer. Bake at 325°F for 60 minutes. Finish cutting diamond or squares through bottom layer. This is important at this point because once syrup is drizzled over, it's too sticky to cut nicely.

Pour warm syrup over cooked pastry making sure to drizzle into cuts. Cool completely.

Laura S. M.

Bobbie's Strawberry Shaped Cookies

INGREDIENTS

6 oz Pkg. Strawberry
  Jell-o®

1/2 C Ground Walnuts

1/2 C Ground Pecans

1 C Coconut, finely
  grated

3/4 C Sweet condensed
  milk

1/2 tsp Vanilla Extract

Red Colored Sugar

1/2 C Almonds, sliced and
  blanched (dyed green
  with food coloring)

DIRECTIONS

In a bowl, combine Jell-o, nuts, and coconut.
Add milk and vanilla, mix well.

Refrigerate for 1 hour.

Use approximately a spoonful and shape into
a strawberry.

Roll in red sugar and top with two almond
slivers to make leaves.

Dry on waxed paper.

Store in tins.

Can be made ahead of time and frozen
for up to one month.

Caramel Lasagna Dessert

INGREDIENTS

1 package Salted Caramel Brownie Oreos® (or plain Oreos®)

6 TB melted butter

1 package (8 oz) softened cream cheese

1/4 cup sugar

2 TB cold milk

3-1/4 cups cold milk

2 tubs (12 oz) Cool Whip®

1 package (5.9 oz) instant caramel pudding (or chocolate)

1/2 bag (11 oz) melted Kraft® Caramel Bits

1-1/2 cup mini chocolate chips

DIRECTIONS

1. Crush the package of cookies into fine crumbs with a food processor or zip to plastic bag and rolling pin.

2. Add butter and mix with fork. Press crumbs into bottom of 9x13 baking pan and refrigerate.

3. Whip or mix cream cheese until fluffy, add sugar, 2TB milk and keep mixing. Add half the melted caramel bits for flavor and stir in one tub of Cool Whip®. Spread over refrigerated crust.

4. Combine box of pudding with 3-1/4 cups of cold milk. Mix until thick and spread over previous layer. Wait five minutes for it to firm up.

5. Spread a tub of Cool Whip® over the top. Drizzle remaining melted caramel over it and sprinkle mini chocolate chips.

6. Freeze for one hour and serve or refrigerate for 4 hours and serve.

Erin L., Strongsville, Ohio

Crepes & Strawberry Puree

INGREDIENTS

Crepe Ingredients:

2 cups milk

4 eggs

3 Tbsp butter, melted

1 Tbsp sugar

1 tsp vanilla

1/2 tsp salt

1-1/2 cups flour, sifted

PUREE INGREDIENTS

Strawberries

Splash of water

Splash of lemon juice

Sugar to taste

DIRECTIONS

Combine all ingredients in a blender until smooth.

Pour 1/4 cup batter in nonstick pan on medium-low heat and swirl to form a good, large circle. Cook 1-2 minutes each side until lightly browned.

Fill with yogurt, fruit, etc. and roll up.

Top with strawberry puree.

Dumped Angel Food Cake

INGREDIENTS

2-3 Angel Food Cakes

2 Packages Gelatin

2 Tubs Whipped topping

Flavors of gelatin at discretion. We've always used sugar free because it tastes more refreshing that way.

DIRECTIONS

Time assembling: about 5 minutes

Shred the angel food cake by hand. Does not have to be perfect (that makes it more fun).

Prepare orange and red gelatin, sometimes some green, lime flavored.

As much whipped topping to make it as moist, to your liking.

Shred 2-3 of these cakes, dump some chopped gelatin into a large bowl. Add about 2 tubs whipped topping (again, by judgement). Mix it with a spatula so it's a chunky cold mess.

Served at family reunions is always a hit! Just keep it shaded on ice for a longer lifespan. Super cheap and easy to make.

"Still delicious, super easy, and very light to eat on the hottest of summers."

Ms. Emily Jane V.

Grandma's Aggression Cookies

INGREDIENTS

1-1/2 C firmly packed brown sugar

3 sticks butter, softened

3 C old fashioned rolled oats

1-1/2 tsp. baking soda

1-1/2 C unsifted all-purpose flour

White sugar to dip glass

DIRECTIONS

Preheat oven to 350°F

Beat together the sugar & butter until smooth.

Add rolled oats, flour, & baking soda.

Knead & squeeze together.

Form dough in small balls (1 teaspoon size).

Place on ungreased baking sheet.

Butter bottom of small glass, dip in sugar, and press cookies flat.

Bake 10-12 minutes.

Let cool on baking sheet a few minutes before removing to wax or parchment paper.

Makes 7 1/2 dozen

Grandma Bean's Apple Dumplings

INGREDIENTS

2 Flour

1-1/4 tsp Baking Powder

1 T Butter

3/4 tsp Salt

Milk, as needed

8 Apples

1/4 C Sugar

DIRECTIONS

Sift dry ingredients into a bowl.

Cut in butter.

Add enough milk to make stiff dough.

Peel and cut apples into pieces.

Divide the dough in half. Roll out on a floured board and cut each piece into 4 squares.

Put pieces from half an apple in the center of squares and bring dough around apple pieces and pinch dough together.

Drop into a pot of boiling water. Cook for 20-25 minutes.

Pot must have a tight fitting lid or dumplings will be heavy. About 5-10 minutes before they are done.

I add the extra apple pieces to the pot. When done, serve with milk and sugar on top.

Makes 8 servings.

"My grandmother would serve these as a meal during the Great Depression, but we always enjoyed them as a child."

Paula H., Niles

Grandma's Chocolate Dessert

DIRECTIONS

1st Layer - Crust
1 stick of melted butter
1 C of flour
3T of powdered sugar
1/4 C of chopped nuts (I prefer peanuts)

Mix above together and spread on the bottom of a 9x13 pan. Bake at 325°F for 20 min. and cool completely.

2nd Layer
8oz of cream cheese
1 C of powdered sugar

Cream above together on high speed until fluffy. Fold in 1 C of Cool Whip (save remaining Cool Whip for 4th Layer). Spread on top of crust.

3rd Layer
2 1/2 C of milk
1 large package of chocolate instant pudding

Beat above and gently spread across the 2nd layer

4th Layer
Top with remaining Cool Whip®

Refrigerate until ready to serve and enjoy!

Grandma's Devil's Food Chocolate Chip Bundt Cake

- -

INGREDIENTS

1 package of Boxed
Devil's Food Cake Mix

4 Eggs

1/2 C of Warm Water

1/2 C of Cooking Oil

8 oz. Sour Cream

1 Small Box of Chocolate
Instant Pudding

12 oz. Bag of Semi-
Sweet Chocolate Chips

DIRECTIONS

Mix all ingredients well, either by hand or by mixer at medium speed.

Spray Bundt pan with cooking oil spray.

Bake in 350 F degree oven for 1 hour.

Beth W., Eaton, Ohio

Mom's Soft Oatmeal Cookies

- -

INGREDIENTS

3/4 C Shortening

1 tsp Baking Soda

1 C Brown or White
    Sugar

1/4 tsp Salt

2 Eggs

1-1/2 C Flour

1 tsp Vanilla

2 C Oatmeal

1 C Sour Milk (To
    make sour milk, mix 1
    teaspoon lemon juice
    with 1 cup milk.)

DIRECTIONS

Preheat oven to 425 degrees F.

Cream the shortening and sugar together;
add eggs and vanilla. Mix until smooth.

Add the sour milk in which the baking soda
has been dissolved, then flour, salt and
oatmeal.

Mix thoroughly, and drop by teaspoonfuls
onto ungreased cookie sheets.

Bake at 425 degrees until done (7 - 10
minutes). Do not over-bake; check bottoms
to be sure that cookies are not burnt.

Cookies will be soft when done, not crispy.

My Mom's Lemon Cheese Dainties

INGREDIENTS

1 pkg 8 oz Cream
  Cheese

1 C Butter

1 C Sugar

1-1/2 tsp Lemon Extract

2 C Flour

DIRECTIONS

1. Preheat oven to 325 degrees F.

2. Cream the cream cheese, butter, sugar, and lemon extract.

3. Add the flour and mix.

4. Drop batter by small teaspoons onto cookie sheet and flatten with a fork or a glass.

5. Dust with colored sugar (my mom made these every Christmas and dusted them with green and red sugar)

6. Bake for 15-20 min.

Sharon D., Springboro

No Bake Oreo® Cake

INGREDIENTS

35 Crushed Oreos®

1 Stick of Butter (softened)

1-8oz Cream Cheese (softened)

1 C Powdered Sugar

1-12oz. Cool Whip® (can use extra for more creamy)

3 C Milk

1 Small Box Instant Vanilla Pudding

1 Small Box Instant Chocolate Pudding

DIRECTIONS

Crush Oreos® and combine with softened butter and mix with your hands. Press and spread evenly into a greased 9 X 12 pan.

Mix sugar, softened cream cheese and 1/2 Cool Whip® with a mixer until well-blended and pour mixture over Oreo® layer.

Blend both boxes of instant pudding mixes with milk and pour into pan.

Top with the remaining Cool Whip® (or more if desired

Nut Milk Chia Seed Pudding

INGREDIENTS

1 C Nuts (almonds or
    cashews work best)

3 C Purified Water

2 Dates

3/4 tsp Vanilla Extract

1/4-1/2 tsp Sea Salt

3/8-1/4 C Chia Seeds

DIRECTIONS

Add all ingredients except chia seeds to a strong blender and blend until smooth. Pour mixture into a glass or ceramic bowl or dish. Add chia seeds and mix well. Set in refrigerator to gel. Every 30 minutes or so stir the mixture to distribute chia seeds evenly throughout the pudding. It will gel completely in a few hours.

Serve as is or top with fruit, maple syrup, honey, fruit preserves, cocoa powder or cocoa nibs, shredded coconut, cinnamon, or other toppings of choice.

Janet L., Lakewood

Peanut Butter Buckeyes

INGREDIENTS

8 ounces semisweet or bittersweet chocolate chips or bar

2 1/2 cups confectioners' sugar

1 cup smooth peanut butter (Jif® or Skippy® works well)

1/4 teaspoon salt

6 tablespoons unsalted butter, melted

1/2 teaspoon vanilla

DIRECTIONS

Line a cookie sheet with waxed paper.

Beat the confectioners' sugar, peanut butter, butter, vanilla and salt with an electric mixer in a medium bowl until well combined.

Roll 2 teaspoons of peanut butter mixture into balls, and place on baking sheet.

Refrigerate until firm, about 20 minutes.

Melt chocolate in a double boiler over medium-low heat to prevent scorching the chocolate.

Skewer each peanut butter ball with a toothpick for easy handling and dip the ball into the melted chocolate. Leave a portion of peanut butter exposed on top of the buckeye.

Dip the rest of the peanut butter balls in the melted chocolate, and place on the wax paper lined baking sheet again.

Place in refrigerator until peanut butter is firm and chocolate is set.

Store in airtight container in refrigerator.

Peanut Butter Chocolate Chip Bars

INGREDIENTS

1 cup peanut butter

1 cup softened butter

1-1/2 cups brown sugar

1 to 2 cups rolled oats

1 to 2 cups squash puree

2 eggs

2 cups all-purpose flour

3 cups chocolate chips

DIRECTIONS

Mix first 5 ingredients with electric mixer until smooth.

Add 2 eggs, one at a time and mix well.

Add 2 cups flour and mix until smooth.

Stir in chocolate chips.

Pour batter into lined cake pan, or cup cake pan.

Bake at 350°F for approx. 20 minutes.

Pumpkin Tea Cake

- -

INGREDIENTS

1 2/3 cups all-purpose flour

1-1/2 teaspoons baking powder

1/2 teaspoon baking soda

1 tablespoon + 2 teaspoons ground cinnamon

2 teaspoons freshly grated nutmeg

1/4 teaspoon ground cloves

1 cup + 2 tablespoons pumpkin or squash puree (canned or homemade)

1 8oz block of cream cheese (room temperature, cut into small cubes)

1 cup vegetable oil

1 1/3 cups sugar

3/4 teaspoon salt

2 large eggs

2 tablespoons sugar for topping

DIRECTIONS

Preheat the oven to 325°F. Lightly butter the bottom and sides of a 9x5 inch loaf pan.

Sift or whisk together the flour, baking powder, baking soda, cinnamon, nutmeg, and cloves.

In another bowl, beat together the pumpkin puree, oil, cream cheese, sugar, and salt on medium speed (or by hand--that's how I did it) until well mixed. Add the eggs one at a time, mixing well after each addition. Scrape down the sides of the bowl. On low speed, add the flour mixture and beat until just combined. Scrape down the sides again, then beat on medium speed for 5 to 10 seconds to make a smooth batter. The batter should have the consistency of a thick purée. Make sure not to overmix, or you will end up with a coarse, tough crumb.

Transfer the batter to the prepared loaf pan. Sprinkle the top evenly with half the topping sugar, and then the rest of the topping sugar. Bake until a tester emerges clean from the center, about 1 hour (I left mine in a bit longer, and it was still ever so slightly underbaked).

Let cook in the pan on a wire rack for about 20 minutes. Then invert the cake onto the rack, turn right side up, and let cool completely. Serve at room temperature. The cake will keep, well wrapped, at room temperature for 4 days or in the refrigerator for about 1 week.

Pumpkin Wonder Cookies

INGREDIENTS

1-1/2 C Real Butter, softened

2 C Packed brown sugar

1 C White Sugar

1 (15-ounce) Can Pumpkin Puree

1 Egg

1 tsp Vanilla Extract

4 C Almond Flour

2C Quick-Cooking Oats

2 tsp Ground Cinnamon

2 tsp Baking Soda

1 tsp Baking Powder

1 tsp Salt

1 C Dark Chocolate Chips

1 C Butterscotch Chips

DIRECTIONS

1. Preheat oven to 375 degrees F.

2. Beat butter, brown sugar, and white sugar together in a bowl until creamy. Add pumpkin, egg, and vanilla extract; beat until smooth.

3. Mix almond flour, oats, cinnamon, baking soda, baking powder, and salt in a separate bowl.

4. Stir dry ingredients into creamed butter mixture until combined. Fold butterscotch and dark chocolate chips into batter.

5. Drop 1 to 2 tablespoons batter for each cookie onto a baking sheet.

6. Bake in the preheated oven until the edges of each cookie appear lightly brown, 10 to 12 minutes.

Yields 6 to 7 dozen

Christina H. B., Wooster

Red, White, and Blue Trifle

INGREDIENTS

Any prepared white cake, or make your own

2 Pints Fresh Strawberries

1 Pint Fresh Blueberries

1 Pint Fresh Blackberries

2 C Pitted Cherries

1 Package Vanilla Pudding, or make your own

Whipped Cream, or Whipping Cream to whip yourself

DIRECTIONS

Best if prepared a day before serving.

Wash and remove stems from blueberries, strawberries, and cherries. Wash blackberries and pit cherries if using fresh. Slice strawberries into a large bowl, add remaining fruit, and mix gently. Set aside.

Prepare pudding and chill in fridge. Prepare cake and cool completely. Give the fruit another gentle stir - the idea is to let some of the juice settle in the bowl.

In a trifle bowl or any large deep glass bowl, break about 1/3 of completely cooled cake into chunks and place in bottom of bowl. Add about 1/3 of the fruit, top with 1/3 of the pudding. Continue to layer in the same manner, ending with cake. Drizzle any fruit juice left over the top. You can also drizzle a little brandy or rum over the top and around the edges if you like.

Cover and refrigerate. Top with whipped cream prior to serving.

Rhubarb Custard Cake

INGREDIENTS

1 Box Yellow Cake Mix

4 C Chopped Rhubarb

1 C Granulated Sugar

1 Pint Whipping Cream
(2 cups)

DIRECTIONS

Prepare batter for cake mix according to package directions & pour into greased and floured 9x13 pan.

Dump the chopped rhubarb on cake batter.

Sprinkle the sugar on top of the rhubarb.

Pour the whipping cream (un-whipped) over the sugar.

Bake at 350 degrees F for 60-65 minutes, until cake springs back when lightly touched.

Cream, sugar, and rhubarb sink to the bottom, forming a custard.

Makes 1-18 servings (depending on how you cut it)!

Serve warm.

Lisa M., Streetsboro

Rolled Butter Cookies

INGREDIENTS

1 cup butter, soft

1 cup sugar

1 egg

2 Tbsp milk

1 tsp baking powder

1/2 tsp salt

1/2 tsp baking soda

1 tsp vanilla

3 cups flour (plus working flour)

DIRECTIONS

Preheat oven to 400 degrees F.

Cream the butter. Gradually add the sugar and cream them together well.

Blend in the egg, milk, baking powder, baking soda, vanilla, and salt.

Gradually add the flour, and mix well.

Roll out on floured surface, and cut into desired shapes.

Place on parchment. Sprinkle with colored sugar.

Bake for 11-14 minutes, then cool on a wire rack. Clean produce. Peel the outside of onion. It's OK to cut the onion into halves or

Secret Family Recipe Chocolate Chip Cookies

- -

INGREDIENTS

2 cups shortening

2 cups dark brown
  sugar

1 cup granulated sugar

4 cups all-purpose flour

4 eggs

1 tsp salt

2 tsp baking soda

2 tsp vanilla

24 oz. bag chocolate
  chips

DIRECTIONS

Cream shortening, sugar, and vanilla. Add eggs. beat well. Slowly add dry ingredients and combine.

Drop by the tablespoonful on ungreased cookie sheet. Bake at 350°F for 12 minutes or until lightly golden brown.

Stacie G., Rocky River

S'mores Bars

- -

INGREDIENTS

7 - 1.45 oz. Dark Choco-
late Bars

2-1/2 Packs of Organic
Graham Crackers

1-1/2 12 oz. Bags of Semi-
Sweet Chocolate Chips

1 tsp Vanilla Extract

1 Stick of Butter

9 cups Miniature Marsh-
mallows, divided

EQUIPMENT

Culinary torch

9x13 pan

Parchment paper

DIRECTIONS

Line a 9x13 inch pan with parchment paper.
Lay 6-7 dark chocolate bars next to each
other so that you create a bed of chocolate. Warm the bed of chocolate in the
oven just long enough to slightly soften.
Do not melt completely. Once softened,
remove from oven.

In a large bowl, break the sheets of graham
crackers into halves and then into fourths
creating bite sized pieces. Toss the graham
crackers with 1 1/2 cups of miniature marshmallows and set aside.

In a double broiler or microwave oven, melt
the chocolate chips and vanilla extract.

In a separate double broiler, melt the stick
of butter and 4 cups of miniature marshmallows. If using a double broiler, be certain
to melt the chocolate and the marshmallows
on low heat.

Remove from heat and mix the chocolate
mixture with the marshmallow/butter mixture.

Combine the chocolate/marshmallow mixture with the graham crackers and coat
well.

Spread evenly over the bed of chocolate
and press down. Spread the top with 3-1/2
cups of miniature marshmallows and use
the culinary torch to roast the marshmallows. The more roasted, the better.

Let the s'mores set in the refrigerator
for 40 minutes to 1 hour. These are best
served at room temperature.

Strawberry Rhubarb Baked Oatmeal

- -

DIRECTIONS

2 C/3-6 stalks/8-9 oz Rhubarb, thinly sliced

3 C/16 oz Strawberries, sliced

In a mixing bowl whisk together:

> 2 Eggs, large*
>
> 1/4 C Flaxseed, ground
>
> 1/2 C Sweetener of your choice
>
> 13 oz Can Coconut Milk
>
> 1-1/4 C Milk, dairy or non-dairy
>
> 4 C Rolled oats, old-fashioned
>
> 1 tsp Seaweed, each - dulse flakes and wakame
>
> 1 tsp Baking Powder*
>
> 1 tsp Baking Soda
>
> 1 tsp Salt

Pour the egg mixture over the fruit and stir gently to combine
Sprinkle over the top with:

> 1/4 C Brown Sugar

Bake 350 F for 45 minutes, or until a toothpick comes out clean in the middle. Serve with milk, cream, yogurt or ice cream for a dessert.

* Note - The day before serving put; fruit in dish, cover withplastic wrap and refrigerate; mix oatmeal mixture except * items, refrigerate in bowl; in the morning stir in * items and finish recipe for quicker assembly when you have overnight guests.

Cindy L., South Charleston

These cookies are going to be huuuge!

INGREDIENTS

2 c. unbleached flour

1-1/4 c. cake flour (preferably King Arthur brand)

2 tsp. baking powder, 1/4 tsp. baking soda

2 sticks (1 cup) cold unsalted butter cubed

2/3 c. packed light brown sugar

2/3 c. granulated sugar

2 c. dark chocolate chips

1 c. coarsely chopped walnuts

2 large eggs (lightly beaten)

DIRECTIONS

1.) Line a 9x13 glass dish with wax paper. Set aside. This dish will be utilized to place the formed cookie dough balls into the freezer. You can cover them if you'd like but it's not necessary.
2.) Use a large bowl to sift together the flours, baking powder, baking soda, and salt. Set aside.
3.) Using a large hand mixer or stand mixer, cream the butter for 30-60 seconds just until the cubes lose their shape.
4.) Combine sugars and pour into the stand mixer bowl. Mix for 30-60 seconds until creamed.
5.) Incorporate walnuts and chocolate chips into the creamed mixture.
6.) Add lightly beaten eggs until combined.
7.) Use your hands to break up any large portions of butter. Be careful not to handle too much as this will soften the butter up. The dough will look crumbly but when squeezed, it will look cohesive.
8.) Form 6-8 dough balls and place in the 9x13 glass dish.
9.) Set the glass dish (uncovered) into the freezer for a minimum of 1-1/2 hours. These dough balls can stay in your freezer, uncovered for up to 1 week before baking.
10.) When ready to bake, place parchment paper on lipped cookie tray. Stagger 4 onto the cookie sheet and bake for exactly 26 minutes (depending on your oven).
****IMPORTANT STEP: Take 1 lipped cookie sheet, place it upside down, then place the other cookie sheet with the parchment paper on top-this prevents quick browning and burning. The cookies will have golden spots edged and will be somewhat doughy on the inside when fully baked.
11.) Once baked, let cool completely. Best when eaten the next day or when cooled, unless you like ooey, gooey goodness.

Breads

Best Banana Bread

Honey Zucchini Bread

Janice's Zucchini Bread

Pepperoni Rolls

Zucchini Bread

Best Banana Bread

- -

INGREDIENTS

1/3 C Flour

1 tsp Baking Soda

8 T Butter, melted

1 tsp Vanilla

2/3 C White Sugar

2 Eggs

2-3 T Milk

DIRECTIONS

Mix all ingredients and spread into 9x9 pan.

Bake 350 degrees F, until golden brown.

May add chocolate chips or blueberries (optional ingredients)

Honey Zucchini Bread

- -

INGREDIENTS

3 Eggs

1/4 C Oil

1-1/2 C Honey

3 C Shredded Raw
   Zucchini

3 tsp Baking Powder

1-3/4 tsp Baking Soda

3 tsp Cinnamon

1 tsp Salt

3 tsp Vanilla

1/8 tsp Orange oil
   (optional)

3 C Flour

1 C Chopped Nuts
   (optional)

DIRECTIONS

Beat eggs, then add honey and oil and beat
for one minute.

Add flour, baking powder, soda, cinnamon,
salt, vanilla, and nuts. Blend all with mixer
slowly & then medium speed till well blended.

Stir in zucchini until well mixed. Pour into 2
greased, lightly floured loaf pans or seven
mini loaf pans.

Bake 45 minutes to 1 hr. depending on your
oven and size of pans at 325°F.

Test with toothpick till comes out clean.

This recipe has already been adjusted for
baking with honey. Recipe may be doubled.

Valerie W.

Janice's Zucchini Bread

INGREDIENTS

3 Eggs

2 C Sugar

3/4 C Cooking Oil

1 T Vanilla

3 C Flour

3 tsp Cinnamon

1 tsp Salt

1 tsp Soda

2 C Grated Zucchini

1/2 C Raisins (optional)

1/2 C Chopped Nuts
(optional)

DIRECTIONS

Beat eggs until frothy. Add sugar. Beat until creamy. Add oil and vanilla. Blend dry ingredients with zucchini. Beat on medium speed for one minute. Fold in raisins and nuts.

Pour into two greased loaf pans.

Bake one hour in 350 degree oven.

"Janice's Tip: This bread is delicious as is, but if you want to make it just a bit more sweet, put a streusel topping over it prior to baking. The topping is made with 1/2 C pre-made baking mix; 1/2 C Brown Sugar; 1/2 t Cinnamon; 2 t Butter. Cut butter into dry mixture and crumble over the bread prior to baking. If you do grow your own zucchini, you can shred up the two cups required for the recipe, place it in freezer bags, then thaw and make this bread in the winter. It's even more delicious then."

Pepperoni Rolls

INGREDIENTS

2 T yeast

1/2 C. lukewarm water

2 C. milk

1 T. sugar

4-5 C. flour

1 t salt

1/4 C. olive oil

pepperoni

mozzarella cheese
(Parmesan & Romano
added to blend is
optional)

DIRECTIONS

Dissolve yeast in lukewarm water. Warm milk for 2 minutes in the microwave. Add sugar and milk to the yeast mixture and let sit until yeast bubbles up.

Mix in 2 cups of flour and oil into the yeast mixture.

Add salt.

Mix in remaining flour until dough is able to be handled. Knead either by hand or with dough hook of mixer for about 5 minutes.

Form a ball with the dough and place in a bowl that has been greased with olive oil. Cover and let rise for 45 minutes or rapid rise in warm oven to double in size.

Divide dough into 4 portions and roll each portion out separately and layer with toppings. Cut with a pizza wheel for either crescent roll or rectangular shape and roll the dough around the toppings.

Let rise again for about 1/2 hour while oven is preheating to 425 degrees. Bake for 20 minutes or until browned and hollow sounding when knocking on roll.

Immediately from the oven (very important), smother tops with butter and some Italian seasonings and garlic to the tops.

"Enjoy!"

Barbara H.

Zucchini Bread

INGREDIENTS

3 Eggs

1 C Oil

2 1/2 C Sugar

2 C Grated Zucchini

2 tsp Cinnamon

1 tsp Salt

1 tsp Baking Soda

1/4 tsp Baking Powder

3 C Unsifted Flour

1 C Chopped Walnuts

DIRECTIONS

Beat eggs until foamy. Gradually add oil and sugar. Add zucchini, cinnamon, salt, baking soda, and baking powder. Mix well.

Gradually blend in flour.

Fold in chopped walnuts.

Pour into 2 greased 9 inch by 5 inch bread pans.

Bake at 350 degrees F for 1 hour.

Freezes well!

Make a lot in the summer and enjoy your bountiful zucchini harvest all winter long.

Dressings & Accompaniments

Avocado Lemon Salad Dressing

Caramelized Onions - Crockpot

Maple Balsamic Dressing

Roasted Red Pepper Relish

Tofu Mayonnaise

Avocado Lemon Salad Dressing

INGREDIENTS

1 Ripe Avocado, Mashed

1 C Extra Virgin Olive Oil

1/4 C Fresh Lemon Juice

1/4 C Apple Cider
 Vinegar

2 T Dried Cilantro
 (or a small bunch
 of chopped fresh
 cilantro)

2 T Garlic Powder (or
 1 clove fresh garlic,
 chopped finely)

2 T Honey

Salt and Pepper to taste

DIRECTIONS

Blend all ingredients together and serve with salad or Cajun / spicy dishes / hot wings as a healthier ranch substitute.

Caramelized Onions - Crockpot

DIRECTIONS

Place in a Crockpot:

> 8 lbs Onion, sliced (using a mandolin slicer works well)
>
> 1 Stick Butter or other fat
>
> Bell Peppers, optional
>
> Mushrooms, optional

Cooking options to try with your specific Crockpot:

Set to high, lid on, until onions are translucent. Set to low, remove lid, cook overnight.

> Set on low, lid on, for 15 hours

Variables: Crockpot, onion type, humidity, etc. Experiment and find what works.

Cool then prepare for the freezer in portions you like. Use a straight sided mason jar any size jelly/pint/1-1/2 pint and freeze.

Uses: Caramelized onions with everything from burgers to potato salad, over mashed potatoes or almost anything!

Cindy L., South Charleston

Maple Balsamic Dressing

- -

INGREDIENTS

1/2 C Olive Oil

1/4 C Balsamic Vinegar

1/4 C Real Maple Syrup

2 T Brown Mustard

Salt and Pepper

DIRECTIONS

Put all ingredients into a mason jar with lid.

Shake it up.

Roasted Red Pepper Relish

INGREDIENTS

3 red bell peppers

1 small or medium onion
  (red or yellow)

10 cloves of garlic

10 habaneros

olive oil

1 lemon

red wine vinegar

salt

pepper

(optional) greens: either
  cilantro, parsley or
  kale

DIRECTIONS

Clean produce. Peel the onion. It's OK to cut the onion into halves or quarters, as that can help peeling.

In a bowl, cover peppers, onion and garlic with olive oil. Salt and pepper. Cover the produce completely with the oil to protect it.

[TIP: Form a circle with the bell peppers, then pile the rest of the smaller ingredients in the middle. This prevents the smaller ones, particularly the habaneros, from roasting faster than the big peppers.}

You can let it cool before you handle it. Drain the water and remove the seeds from the peppers and remove any stems. If it is easy, remove the white parts the seeds cling to.

Put the peppers, onions and garlic in your food processor. Add your greens. Dash in some red wine vinegar. Blend until desired consistency.

Toss the blended relish back onto the bowl where you had the olive oil so you don't waste the extra that was at the bottom. Squeeze in the lemon. Stir well.

Enjoy!

Refrigerate leftover portions. The vinegar and lemon will both give it flavor and help to preserve it longer. Roast in the oven at 375F for 30 minutes.

Erik C.

Tofu Mayonnaise
Makes about 2 cups

- -

DIRECTIONS

Combine in a blender:

I lb. Tofu, firm preferred but soft is okay

2 Cloves Garlic, minced

2 T Soy Sauce

2 Lemons, juiced (about 1/4 c.)

1 tsp Salt

4 tsp Coriander, ground

1 Handful Parsley, fresh or 1/2 c. dried

Store in refrigerator. Use to make tuna salad so good no one will know the traditional mayo is missing!

Beverages

Bourbon Buckeye Cocktail

Cinnamon Maple Whiskey Sour

Gingerbread Smoothie

Grandma Jean's Iced Coffee

Margaritas in Minutes

Bourbon Buckeye Cocktail

INGREDIENTS

2 packets hot chocolate mix

12 oz. hot water

2 oz. Bourbon of your choice

1 tsp. melted peanut butter, plus more to drizzle on top

whipped cream

DIRECTIONS

Pour hot chocolate packets into cup and stir in hot water and bourbon.

Melt the peanut butter for 30 seconds in the microwave, so it's easier to blend. Then mix in peanut butter.

Top each cup with whipped cream. Drizzle with extra melted peanut butter.

Cinnamon Maple Whiskey Sour

- - - - - - - - - - - - - - - - - - -

INGREDIENTS

1-1/2 ounces (3 tablespoons) bourbon of choice

1 ounce (2 tablespoons) fresh lemon juice

2 to 4 teaspoons maple syrup, to taste (I like 3 teaspoons, which is the equivalent of 1/2 ounce or 1 tablespoon. Also if you can get local Ohio maple syrup that is what I prefer)

Pinch of ground cinnamon, optional

DIRECTIONS

Fill a cocktail shaker or mason jar about two-thirds full with ice. Pour in the bourbon, lemon juice, maple syrup and a pinch of ground cinnamon. Securely fasten the lid and shake well.

Pour fresh ice into your cocktail glass and strain the cold whiskey sour mixture into the glass.

Pam L., Cuyahoga Falls

Gingerbread Smoothie

- -

INGREDIENTS

2 frozen bananas

1/2 teaspoon cinnamon

1/8 teaspoon ground
   cloves

1/4 teaspoon ginger

1/8 teaspoon nutmeg

1 teaspoon vanilla

1 cup milk

DIRECTIONS

Blend all ingredients in a blender or
smoothie maker.

Enjoy!

Grandma Jean's Iced Coffee

INGREDIENTS

2 1/2 cups coffee,
  brewed strong

2 cups half-and-half

1/2 cup sugar

3 cups milk

1-1/2 tsp vanilla

DIRECTIONS

Mix all together and freeze.

Thaw 1-1/2 hours before needed

Courtney K.

Margaritas in Minutes

INGREDIENTS

1 12oz. can frozen limeade

1 12 oz. can or bottle of light beer

12 oz. tequila of your choice (I like a Reposado in this recipe)

12 oz. water

4 ounces Cointreau or Gran Mariner

zest of one lime (optional)

DIRECTIONS

Combine all ingredients in a pitcher and stir to mix thoroughly..

Pour over ice-filled salt-rimmed glasses.

Garnish with a lime wedge

Enjoy!